I, Immigrant

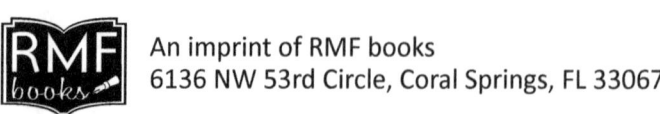 An imprint of RMF books
6136 NW 53rd Circle, Coral Springs, FL 33067

E-mail: contact@rmfbooks.com
        rmf@rmfbooks.com

1st Edition by RMFbooks, 2015

The rights of Umberto Fabbri as author have been asserted in accordance with the Copyright, Designs and Patents Act 1988.

International Cataloguing Information in Publication
Fabbri, Umberto

I, Immigrant
Umberto Fabbri - Florida - US

For information about bulk discounts or to purchase copies of this book, please contact RMFbooks at 954-345-9790 or contact@rmfbooks.com

Translation by Angela Milanese from original Portuguese-language edition with revision by Thais Ortega and Jennifer Jensen

Cover by Adhemar Ribeiro and André Stenico

Manufactured in the United States of America

253 p;

I,
immigrant

Contents

To Immigrate 7

Chapter 1º - Sweets and Memories 9

Chapter 2º - My Mother 23

Chapter 3º - Life Teaches You 31

Chapter 4º - The United States............................41

Chapter 5º - The Interview 51

Chapter 6º - A Friendly Conversation.....................55

Chapter 7º - The Beginning 61

Chapter 8º - Changes 65

Chapter 9º - Starting My New Job 71

Chapter 10º - Moving On 79

Chapter 11º - Some Thoughts 93

Chapter 12º - Always Learning 99

Chapter 13º - Unexpected News 107

Chapter 14º -My Home 113

Chapter 15º - Matters of the Heart 117

Chapter 16º - Values 127

Chapter 17º - Guava Paste, Once Again 133

Chapter 18º -A Bizarre Client Interview 141

Chapter 19º - Proposal 153

Chapter 21º - A Challenging Start 157

Chapter 22º - New Clients 167

Chapter 23º - New Commitments 175

Chapter 24º - The Excluded 183

Chapter 25º - Special Day 189

Chapter 26º - Special Day – A Curious Fact 197

Chapter 27º - Special Day – Ethics Above All...........209

Chapter 28º -A Big Family 217

Chapter 29º - Happiness, Without Comparisons 225

Chapter 30º - In Love 233

Chapter 31º - Life History.....................................243

Chapter 32º - I, Immigrant 251

To Immigrate

Behind my house, there is a lake that cuts across the large residential community where I live in Florida. The area is filled with gorgeous animals attracted by the warm and pleasant climate. They do not appear at the same time, but take turns, arriving throughout the four seasons of the year. Fascinating and enchanting, these splendid creatures delight us with their unique displays of nature's perfection.

The lake, teeming with fish, serves as a natural habitat to several types of birds. Ducks and squirrels are also regional residents, while a cornucopia of herons and pelicans migrate from various parts of the country. Striking and diverse, the fauna and flora form a mosaic of harmonious coexistence between native species and seasonal migrants.

One of the most captivating species is the snowbird. Seeking warmer weather and more abundant food, those lovely visitors always arrive in November, and depart in mid-March.

I compare, metaphorically, these beautiful birds to immigrants, who leave their homeland to settle in another nation. Some are searching new opportunities and successes, others are pursuing their dreams, and still others are just seeking their survival, plain and simple.

I, Immigrant explores the pains, experiences, successes and failures of those who brave uncertainty to create a better life on other shores. The main character, Francisco, is a fictitious Brazilian lawyer who moves to the United States filled with hopes and aspirations. Some of the stories presented are based on actual events, but the details are altered to preserve identities.

Our purpose is to craft stories that inspire positive images about our values, and about the way we face our lives, and relate to other people, so that we can "immigrate" to the most dangerous and barren dimension-- our innermost self.

Umberto Fabbri

Coral Springs, June 2015.

CHAPTER 1

Sweets and Memories

I was born in a small town in the São Paulo countryside that had a population of approximately 10,000 inhabitants. Everyone knew each other and, in my innocence, I thought they were happy.

My parents were Catholic and chose my name, Francisco Martins, in honor of their favorite saint. Martins is my father's surname, but Francisco is after the saint of Assisi. I am the only son of a mechanic and a housewife.

My memories of my early childhood are from the 1960s, a time when, for me, a child of five years, life seemed simple and beautiful.

Today I know that our home was very poor, but at that time I had no notion of what wealth, poverty or misery were. In my naivety, I thought everything was as it should be, since I had no knowledge of wealth or luxury. Thus, how could I miss something I did not even know? My father was a mechanic in a very small town, so how could he be rich?

I started to notice that my mother was always in front of a tub filled with clothes which people brought in large bundles. Eventually, I figured out that she washed and ironed clothes to improve the meager income that we had.

As time went by and I got older, I realized that our situation was very difficult. The few toys I had, usually donated by a generous neighbor, were old, some of them broken. But who cared if the cart was missing a wheel or two? My father was a mechanic, wasn't he? Couldn't he fix just about anything?

However, I have very few memories of my father from my childhood. The amount of work in our town did not cover our household expenses. For that reason, he used to visit the neighboring towns in search of more work.

With much struggling, 'we scraped by', as my mother often said.

In my neighborhood, children of my age were scarce and their mothers did not always let them play with me. They called them back into the house when they saw me coming around. I did not understand the reason for this and when I asked my mother, her answers were always evasive. "It's because it's bath time, or lunch time, or dinner time," she would say.

I thought it was odd. Why have a bath in the middle of the

morning, or have a dinner right in the middle of the afternoon?

Little did I know that poverty was viewed with great prejudice and, although I did not realize it, I was the portrait of poverty. I wore second-hand clothes. My toys, when I had them, were mostly old and broken. But why would they care so much about this? Were they not still toys? What was wrong with my clothes? Even though too big for my size or old, were they not clean? Neatly stitched and with all their buttons?

Somehow, my innocence protected me in a time full of prejudice, when people valued others for their appearance, possessions, and power.

It took me a long time to understand that I was living in a very shabby house, one of the few that had not yet been demolished. The owner had died and the property was in the probate process. The heirs had abandoned it. I learned much later that they were quarreling over the fortune that the old owner had accumulated.

But, my God, why fight over an old house?

At that time I had a great friend, at least that was what I thought. He was more than 60 years old. What innocence! How could a person of that age befriend a boy of only five?

Ah, I have such fond memories of Mr. Roberto, a taxi driver. He was one of the neighbors who, in the words of my mother, had already achieved his place in the sun since he had his own car and, even in those difficult times, had managed to get a house of his own.

For me, a little child, Mr. Roberto's home looked very large. It had a "huge" backyard that in reality was very small, but that relative notion of space I only acquired later.

We also had a backyard, but it only had room for a wash tub and perhaps one square meter or so that my mother used to put out the laundry to dry. I played on the sidewalk in front of my home, the door of which was always open. We were not worried that someone would sneak in, after all, who would be interested in stealing anything from a house almost in ruins?

It was in Mr. Roberto's backyard that I found happiness, but I did not really understand the reason for it. Because I was little, my friend's wife, Ms. Lúcia, asked my mother to let me visit them. It was great fun for me because I had a chance to play in the backyard, have dinner with my friend, and best of all, I could spend hours talking to him while we swung in the hammock suspended between large trees.

Little did I know that Ms. Lúcia was actually doing an act of charity, because she knew how hard things were for my mother, who even after washing and ironing all those clothes, was not able to substantially increase our family's income. Food was scarce, especially for two adults and a child. Ms. Lúcia was able to help us, looking after me, so that my mother could work, and by feeding me dinner almost daily.

Dinner at my friend's home was always very good. Besides the delicious food, we had great conversations, and with all the innocence of a child who has just come into this world, a newcomer from God's bosom, I asked Mr. Roberto about everything, while we merrily swung in the hammock.

God, I was so happy! From time to time, after dinner, we savored a piece of guava paste. Oh yes, that was life indeed!

I knew there was no risk that this friend would be called in by his mother, destroying our game, so I enjoyed his companionship as much as I could. I asked him millions of questions which were always answered with care and patience.

One day, I said, "Mr. Roberto, can I ask you a question?"

"Of course, Francisco, ask anything you want."

"Who made this guava paste?"

"It was Ms. Lúcia, why?"

"Are you sure? I thought it was God."

"God? Why would you think that, Francisco?"

"It is because you always thank God for everything you eat."

"Ah! Francisco, you are so creative!"

Mr. Roberto taught me to thank God for all the food

that we had. Obviously, I understood that it was not God who cooked it, but I was sure that He was the one that provided it. In my childhood naivety, I just thought that the food they ate was being sent by God, since it was so different and plentiful! Certainly God was very kind to them because He sent guava paste, fruit, rice, beans and even steak on special occasions.

I used to call Roberto "old man." I heard his wife, who was also my friend, call him that. If she could do it, why couldn't I?

I persisted with more questions regarding our relationship with God. My parents stated that He was in Heaven, which must be a faraway place because we did not always have guava paste and steak.

My mother would say that God was very busy, that our turn would come. But time went by and the much anticipated divine gifts never arrived.

My parents did not attend church regularly, but my mother taught me to pray and to ask our Father in Heaven to protect us and to provide us the things we really needed. I always asked to be able to keep eating guava paste while having good conversations with my old friend as we swung in the hammock.

However, I was soon without my friend, without our conversations in the hammock, without the wonderful guava paste. When one day, I watched this big commotion at his house. People were coming and going, trying to disguise their relentless tears. Someone said, "Don't let the boy watch."

The "old man" was gone forever. I was told that he went to live with God. Maybe they were good friends and perhaps even related, they tried to explain it to me.

Later on, I learned the truth. He had been hired for a drive from which he would never return. A criminal, wanting to steal his car, cowardly shot and murdered him, and then fled in the taxi with some small change that the Old Man had earned that day.

Mr. Roberto was gone and then his wife left our neighborhood too. She fell on hard times, so she went to live with a daughter in another city far away. Their house was left empty; even the hammock was gone.

A year passed, and one day, one of the "heirs" of our house appeared, saying he wanted us to leave the house. I did not understand. Why did he want that old house? My dad said they wanted to tear it down and build a new one. Meanwhile, we were moving somewhere else to wait for the new house to be ready. What a sweet fantasy that was! I thought, one day I would live in a new house like the other children. Maybe then their mothers would let me play with them more often.

In reality, we went to live in a small village, crammed into an even smaller space. In the old house I had a bed; in the new one I had to sleep on a sofa in the living room. But I did not care! Mom said that many people had no home at all. But she believed that one day the government would help us.

That was another dream that would never come true. This so-called "man from the government," who would solve all our problems, never showed up. But my mother heard on the newscast, on a neighbor's radio, that the poor would get help, so we hoped, and waited for the help to come.

After a while, I was enrolled in the local school. "You will study to become someone," my parents used to say. But I didn't understand what they meant. After all, wasn't I someone already? Maybe not. Maybe the school could transform this Francisco "nobody" into somebody.

Off I went, excited to become someone. But the enchantment of those first days did not last long. Back then, teachers were allowed to inflict corporal punishment on children that misbehaved, or who had learning difficulties. To me, it was so hard to understand that bunch of letters and numbers! The teacher, whenever she could, beat me with a cane, which she carried into the classroom with pride, like the scepter of an empress.

Afraid of the blows, I skipped school whenever I could.

My father would leave me at the front door, and I went out through the back gate. Since the school was in a low-income neighborhood, security was not very good. The children often walked barefoot, and like me, wore second-hand clothes. Many of them went to class just to get their free school lunch, which was perhaps their only meal of the day.

I could not understand why the teacher was always giving me beatings in front of my schoolmates, who snickered. My parents never hit me. Why was that happening to me? What did I do wrong? She yelled, "You dumb, stupid boy. You can't do anything right!" Repeating those words, she caned me, to the delight of some classmates and the despair of others, who would undergo the same torture session after mine. I realized then that people could become violent.

Because I fled the school and returned home, my father started to hit me with his old belt. Angrily, he would scold me, "You will not be a slacker, Francisco! If you think you can drop out of school, think again!"

In my bleakest hours, I asked my friend, "Mr. Roberto, I know that God's house must be very good and you must be happy there, but I miss you so much! Why don't you take a trip and come help me?"

Since he did not come, the only solution was to improve my comprehension of those letters, and get those numbers right. That way, I would avoid the spankings, allegedly inflicted for my own good. However, as far I was concerned, those spankings could never do me any good. After attending school for a while, I improved my reading and writing skills and was able to understand the numbers a little better.

One day, my mother arrived home, exulting with joy, saying that our time had finally come.

God helped us, she announced. From now on, we would eat better, and maybe even live in a bigger house, because my father had found a job in a state-owned coffee processing plant. My ingenuous mother, with her limited experience, was convinced that he would have an important position. He would work as a coffee bean sorter.

If that was a very important position, I wouldn't have known, but my mother believed it, and so did I. At that moment, I remembered my friend Mr. Roberto. He must have spoken with God and arranged this job for my father. The only thing missing, to complete my happiness, was the guava paste.

Incidentally, it had been a long time since I had tasted any guava paste. I only remember having thin soup, soup in the winter, soup in the summer, and so on.

"Don't complain, son. At least we have soup," my dad used to say.

But now that my father would receive a steady paycheck, things would change. Hopefully, we would have better meals.

We were euphoric. It was as if we had won the lottery. To make things even better, my father's earnings would allow me to sign up for the dental care program at my school. It was a token fee, but how could we afford to pay a dentist, when we had barely enough to eat? Our solution was to live with cavities, to mouthwash with vinegar and salt to alleviate toothaches, or pull out the rotten teeth.

I was blessed, my mother declared. Due to a genetic predisposition, which we knew nothing about, my teeth had only a few cavities and, amazingly, the dentist did not have to extract any. I suspected that Mr. Roberto had something to do with that too. Maybe he and God had a pleasant conversation, after lunch, while sitting on a hammock in their house's backyard, up in Heaven, and my old friend asked Him for something on my behalf, even if only to spare me the dentist's forceps.

I avoided the forceps, but not the dental drill, a terrible tool of torture according to my classmates, and since no anesthesia was used, I was able to experience for myself how right they were.

Life started to show signs of improvement. At school, between getting good grades or facing the cane, I chose to make the effort required to earn good grades, which also saved me from my father's old belt.

My mother was extremely protective, but at the same time naïve. Perhaps because she had placed all her hopes in me, she treated me as if I were a piece of crystal. I was not allowed to leave the house to play with my schoolmates, or with the children from our street. It was dangerous, she argued, because an accident might happen. As far as she was concerned, it would be better if I stayed indoors, even if I had to play alone, because then no danger from the street would ever hurt me.

To her, the street represented the hard life she had, filled with difficulties and limitations. People often treated her as a lowly laundress, a second-class person, which left her ashamed. Because of her wounded pride, she barely left our house. The visits we did, which of course were on foot, covering long distances, were to my grandparents' or to my aunt's home. Other than that, it was our house that waited for me, day after day.

Some time later, my father, working his heart out, as my mother always said, had saved a little money and managed to pay the first installment on a plot of land in a nearby village. His goal was to eventually build us a house. Yes, life had gotten better. My old friend, Mr. Roberto, must have had considerable influence with God, I thought.

Those were good times because after school I had fun loading bricks for our future home, and since I had no classes on Saturdays and Sundays, I could drive nails into the wood floor. What a joy for us, because we finally would have a home of our own, freeing us from the landlord and from paying rent, which my father paid with great sacrifice, as he always said.

It took almost two years, but the house was finally ready. By that time there had been a military coup d'état in the country, and the Army had declared that life would improve. I remember my mother saying that it was a revolution, and that in large cities, people were fighting in the streets.

Eventually, she claimed, the unrest would settle down and then everything would be better than before. The question that I sometimes asked her was, better for whom? Because the government official I had expected to come and help us when we were almost starving had never appeared. Would those people in uniform be any different?

Time is a blessing because it is the lord of reason. Everything remained exactly the same.

CHAPTER 2

My Mother

Many changes occurred in our lives over a short period of time. We had been living in our new home for a little over four months, when my father suffered a massive heart attack which ended his life. With great sadness, I realized that another person I loved was gone forever.

Perhaps it was the sudden departures that I witnessed as a boy which inspired me to make so many changes in my life later.

It was as if my loved ones had immigrated to a place from which they could never return, nor send me any news about themselves. Maybe the adventure they were now living in this faraway nation, Heaven, did not allow any type of communication with those left behind.

My father, without a doubt, would get there. Hopefully, he would not find Heaven very lonely because he would meet another immigrant, my old friend Mr. Roberto, who would certainly welcome him with open arms and that smile which had always reassured me.

Likely, the two of them would enjoy plenty of delicious food, and would have pleasant conversations, sitting with God, Who must have had a huge hammock, or perhaps several of them, because there are so many people, from so many ages, that immigrated to Heaven.

Those losses made me understand the meaning of the old adage, "All good things must come to an end."

My mother, still very young, who until then had only ever cared for our home, went into total despair after the death of my father, followed by a severe nervous breakdown, which worsened with our financial situation, until we were left without basic resources, such as food and medicine.

Although my father had a regular job when he died, which entitled us to receive a pension, the government took a year and a half to start paying it. The bureaucracy was terrible. My mother had to make several trips to the state capital, using money borrowed from neighbors and relatives, to petition for the release of her pension money.

Over time, I realized that she had started to change. Before, she had been a loving mother, but gradually she became a cold, remote person. She was impatient and extremely severe, making no allowances, especially on my part.

She punished me for anything, hitting me with any object that she could find: broomsticks, a garden hose, a belt that had belonged to my father. Displaying her instability, she eventually made a type of whip out of copper wire; then she used it to inflict her infamous beatings on me.

Unfortunately, this kind of treatment was very common back then. Parents routinely used corporal punishment to discipline their children. Their minds were authoritarian and backwards, their actions in accordance with society's approval. They would beat their children and then brag about it. As I recall, I became the subject of some repeated conversations about discipline and education, in which my mother described the "exemplary" way she "educated" her son. It seemed to me that I was a source of pleasure for torturers, both for those who recounted the tales of my beatings and for those who listened to them.

It was the absence of my father, she argued, that forced her to become both a mother and a father, and so she had to be extra vigilant to ensure that I did not weaken or step out of line. In her ignorance or simple-mindedness, she did not realize that over time the violence caused by her emotional disarray would only deepen the fractures in her soul, and this would eventually lead to insanity.

The situation only worsened. To my mother, taking care of her child simply meant keeping him well nourished.

Since she had never received any warmth or affection from my grandparents, she repeated the behavior which she believed had worked for her, the cold treatment that had made her who she was.

Finally, the pension money arrived. We paid off our many debts, and what remained was put our at interest. Our account was managed by my uncle, who was married to my mother's sister. But that was another disappointment. The money simply vanished like smoke, and with it, our hopes for a better life.

Our only option was to move to a big city, where I could get a job as an office assistant or an office boy, in spite of my young age. With my earnings, her small widow's pension, and the selling of our house, we might have a better life. Or so we hoped.

"Where there's life, there's hope," people say. Thus, filled with our illusions, we went to the state capital, to its huge buildings and busy streets crammed with people and cars. Everything seemed like a dream, and we believed we would be happy. We had experienced so many changes in such a short time. But this change was unique, it carried some promise of happiness. At least that was what I thought.

Our priorities were to first find a place to live and then a public school for me. Money was tight, and we were still waiting for our house to be sold. So, we went to live in an apartment at the rear of a building downtown. It was an extremely impoverished region, filled with tiny hovels, which looked like shacks, one on the top of the other.

I left our home only to go to school, returning immediately after class. A few months later, a family acquaintance, answering my mother's pleas, got me a job as an office boy.

The money from the sale of the house finally arrived, but in the hands of my mother, a person who suffered serious a mental disorder and had numerous debts, it just disappeared. Before long we lost all of it.

I handed over my small office boy's salary to my mother. However, my earnings and her pension were barely enough to cover our housing and food expenses.

My clothes and shoes were second-hand donations from relatives or acquaintances. They were usually too big for me. My shoes were so large they slipped off, and had to be stuffed with newspaper to fill the space around my feet. I was often mocked by classmates and colleagues. One would exclaim, "Big pants!" Another would ask, "Why didn't you grab a shirt from a smaller corpse?" But I could hardly afford to care about fashion or things like that. The important thing was to be fully dressed and with shoes to wear.

I was thirteen years old, and the beatings still happened,

although less frequently. But there were occasions on which, without any rhyme or reason, my mother was over-taken by an uncontrollable rage, becoming a different person, so intense was the fury that possessed her.

On weekends, for fun, I used to play in the streets with a soapbox car. I lived near a cul-de-sac with a downhill slope, ideal for the game. They were rare moments of happiness in those tough times. In my juvenile imagination, those were moments when I could be totally free. While the wooden car gained speed, I felt the wind blowing hard across my face. It was a real glimpse of hope and comfort for someone who had already suffered so much in his short life. Sometimes I felt as if I were gliding through the clouds, oblivious to everything: my poverty, the difficulties with my mother, and the mockery from my peers.

But in one of those adventures, I skinned the fingers of my right hand on the asphalt. It was nothing serious, just harmless kid stuff, as we used to say.

It was nothing serious, but how could I explain that to my mother--explain how I had grated my fingers on the asphalt? Why wasn't I more careful?

My fear of punishment was so strong that I decided to hide my right hand when I was near her. We did not have much physical contact between us, there were no demonstrations of affection or love, so hiding my hand was not a very difficult thing to do. But one day, while I was doing my homework before going to my job, she saw the abrasions around my fingers.

The interrogation started right away.

"What is that? What happened to your hand?" Already terrorized, familiar with her violent outbursts and afraid of a beating, I answered, "It's nothing. I scraped my hand on the asphalt while playing with my soapbox car."

It was enough.

Despite my pleas, the little car was torn into pieces right in front of me, with such fury that it frightened me. Where did she get the strength to break a wooden car in just a few minutes?

So long, goodbye, to my moments of freedom and dreams, those moments when I lived in the heights of my imagination.

But she was not yet satisfied, and when I returned home from an exhausting day making deliveries for work and attending classes, another nasty surprise awaited me. My poor, sick mother approached the couch, which served as my bed, and with her tormenting whip, gave me a painful beating. Breaking my wooden car, my only source of escape, was not enough to appease her wrath.

The years continued to go by, filled with more painful events like that. Until one day, when I was sixteen years old,

I had a sad surprise waiting for me when I got home. My mother was gone. She simply left without saying anything.

No one knew where she had gone, or why she left our home. A neighbor told me that, just days earlier, she had complained about her circumstances, claiming that she was tired of her life, that she could not stand the burden of raising me alone, and that it was an overwhelming responsibility having to worry about money, home, and raising me. Well, that was it. She had a breakdown, abandoned her house, and left me behind. I was alone and scared. I remembered Mr. Roberto and my father. I would have given anything to have them with me.

CHAPTER 3

Life Teaches You

My life got even more complicated. Alone, with only my meager salary as an office boy, I could not make ends meet. Either I could pay the rent or I could buy food, but not both.

I decided to keep paying rent to give myself some time to put my life in order. Besides, I still needed to work and study. Therefore, living in the street was not an option.

I asked my colleagues to help, and they shared their lunches with me so I would have something to eat. But I knew this arrangement would not last. After all, they also had their own financial struggles, and could not afford to feed me forever. In fact, they barely had enough for themselves.

I was starving. Sometimes, a more compassionate neighbor, seeing that I was beginning to lose weight, would give me some bread, rice or any leftover food he could spare. But I urgently needed to do something. I could not continue to live that way.

The solution was to move to a boardinghouse, and after much searching, I found one that seemed decent enough and that I could afford. Best of all, a daily meal was included in the arrangement.

I moved to this new place, hoping to live a little better. It was a large old building. The rooms were rented and shared by three or four people each.

I was placed in a tiny room, slightly larger than a closet. It had no bed, just an old child's mattress placed directly on the floor. The space was so small that the mattress had to be placed crosswise, and even so, I had to sleep with my legs tucked in. Reflecting on my current circumstances, and all the difficulties I had endured, I would remember my father. I could swear I heard his voice, saying "Don't complain Francisco, there are people who don't have even that. Be strong, my son, be brave."

Feeling more encouraged, I tried to control my thoughts, avoiding self-pity. I was content to have a place to live and food to eat. Still, not only did I have to get used to the awful conditions of my room, I also had to struggle mightily to prevent the fleas that infested the place from devouring me. But I managed to beat them! I got a poison so strong that it almost killed me instead of the little bandits.

I won that battle, and I continued to fight the war of survival that I waged every day just to keep working and studying. I really wanted to go to college. My dream was to become a lawyer. I remembered the lawyers responsible for the probate process of my old house. They were dignified people, exuding self-confidence, and I greatly respected and admired them. Certainly, I would be happy as a lawyer. I would wear neat suits instead of second-hand clothes and shoes. I would also have a nice house, where I could shelter my family and entertain friends, putting an end to my loneliness. It was my dream of happiness.

Clearly, I needed a better job. I needed to improve my living conditions. Most of all, I needed a good salary to cover my college tuition and book expenses. I focused on that goal, and after some time, I got a job in a law firm, as an office assistant. It was not much, since it was a low-level position, but the salary was well above the one I currently had. Better yet, I would be dealing directly with law issues, which was the field I wanted to study.

I never complained about my burdens. I understood that if you have had very little, you do not miss the things you never had, or the things you do not even know about. In my job, I always paid careful attention, seeking to learn as much as I could. Often, I heard conversations among the lawyers in the office about their business or vacation trips abroad, to Europe and the United States. I found it fascinating, but at the same time completely foreign to my reality, not just because of the physical distance, but because it was something beyond my imagination. I saw myself as the little guy, struggling daily to achieve my dreams and fulfill my aspirations, so I could not even imagine going outside of Brazil.

My main goal was to attend a good college. Thus, I needed to concentrate on my work and studies. I wanted to have a better life. Poverty is not a crime, but I was determined to prevent it from becoming my permanent destiny. I was motivated, but the challenge was more formidable than I expected. The competition to get into a public university was fierce, so I had to be extremely well prepared.

Life is often cruel for those who are soft, but I have always been strong-willed. I did not give up on things easily, because giving up on things, when you have nothing, means giving up on life, and that was totally unacceptable.

Thus, with much sacrifice, this strong-willed young man was accepted into a public law school. My boss, who had followed my fight to succeed from afar, honored me. He was always paying attention to his most hardworking and committed employees.

He told me, "I believe that you'll need textbooks

for your studies. Our law firm values a college education, and supports the efforts of employees who seek further development. Since you're studying to become a lawyer, we will help you get the resources you'll need."

To me, that was like winning the lottery. Receiving those textbooks and supplies would be a huge cost saving, because they were quite expensive, especially the law textbooks.

With plenty of help, I completed my law degree. The next challenge was to take the Brazilian bar exam. I could not be an attorney until I passed this complex exam, which would get me an admission into the Brazilian Bar Association, as well as my law license. Only then would I be legally entitled to work in my chosen profession. I studied exhaustively for six months and then I took the bar exam. I passed on my first try!

The president of our law firm, who supported not only me, but all the employees who sought to improve their situation, celebrated when he heard about my success. He congratulated me, and using beautiful words of encouragement, he told me about the opportunities available in the firm, which left me deeply moved.

Meanwhile, my salary gradually improved, as well as my standard of living. I left the flea-infested boardinghouse and moved to a small apartment, which was then known as a 'kitchenette'. It had one bedroom, a bathroom and a tiny space for a stove and a fridge, which could barely be considered a kitchen.

I looked for my mother, but I never heard from her again. It was if she had never existed. In a country that is the size of a continent, losing contact with a person is not a very difficult thing to do, especially back then, and especially when a person does not want to be found.

I wondered, sometimes, what I had done wrong. The truth was, she was a sick person, and the death of my father had only made things worse. Eventually, I gave up searching for a logical explanation, because otherwise I would blame myself forever, even for being born. I would not do that to myself. I realized that it was very easy to take the blame for others' mistakes. But time is God's medicine, because it heals everything, and one day I would make my peace with the disappearance of my mother. I needed to move forward. That cycle was finished. After experiencing so many hardships, I was stronger, and I was brave enough to keep going and keep fighting for what I believed.

My new position as an attorney, was very demanding. But the salary, unfortunately, was still too modest to effectively improve my life. The economic situation in the country was chaotic. Brazil, fresh out of a dictatorial regime, was struggling. The vast majority of institutions were totally destroyed or operated with outdated technology.

Our office had trouble finding new clients or even keeping the old ones, because the competition was fierce and unfair at times.

One day, a long-time colleague told me about life in the United States. He said to me, "The United States is the land of opportunity! Whoever goes there has no regrets, because their standard of living is one of the best in the world. It has a good system of education, security, transportation and the quality of life is undeniable."

I started to dream about it. At the same time, I started reading everything I could about this land where, it seemed, everyone had a place in the sun.

I talked to anyone who could give me some information about those people who worked hard but lived in peace. Yes, that was how life should be, I reasoned. I reflected on my own experience. I had become accustomed to working hard since my childhood; life could not be any harsher than it had been already.

One day, out of the blue, Sergio, one of my coworkers, and also my friend, proposed, "Why don't we go there? Let's move to the United States!"

"What do you mean? Move how? How can we leave everything behind?" I replied.

That "everything" I mentioned was almost nothing. Still,

it provided a certain security. Besides, there were language issues, since my knowledge of English was minimal.

I questioned him. "But Sergio, where will we work, and do what?"

He countered, "Don't worry. We can get a job as an assistant gardener, for example. You know how to cut grass, don't you?"

"Yes, I know," I replied. "I just don't want to go backwards. You know how life was tough for me, and how difficult it was to get where I am."

"That is exactly why we must go," he said. "As lawyers, here in Brazil, we can barely pay our bills. Maybe, as regular workers, In the United States, we have a better chance to make it, since we will earn our money in dollars."

"How are we going to get there? What about the visas?"

"We'll go as tourists, like many people do. We'll try to find something to do quickly, and we'll stay on. Afterwards we'll get an extension of the visa, so that we won't be staying there illegally. We'll manage the situation for as long we can, and if nothing comes of it, we'll come back. I have a friend who has been living there for a while. He works in a landscaping business, and I know we can stay with him. He can even help us get a job, since the company where he works is looking for more employees."

He concluded, "We're still very young, and you know,

'Nothing ventured, nothing gained.' So, Francisco, what do you say, shall we go?"

I already knew the answer to Sergio's question. "It can't get any worse than this," I replied. "Let's go!"

CHAPTER 4

The United States

E ager for new opportunities, we made our visa applications. It was not very difficult, since we were employed and would pretend to go on vacation, like any tourist.

We knew that the United States applied serious and strict criteria for issuing the temporary visitor visa. The officials who conducted our interviews at the Consulate were vigilant, but also courteous and polite. We explained that we were going to Florida to visit Disney World. That at least was not a lie, because Mario, our host in the United States, informed us that we would visit Orlando. Anyway, our visas were approved.

We managed to buy our plane tickets for an affordable price. The plane would make a stop in Chile, which would add four more hours to our trip, but that was not a problem.

Finally, the big day arrived. Getting on the plane made

me nervous. My first takeoff ever gave me chills, and tightened my stomach into knots, followed by a lot of prayers. Throughout the journey, I imagined what my new life would be like.

I felt nostalgic. Flying up in the skies, I remembered my parents, my friend Mr. Roberto, and my childhood. I could not figure out whether the tightness in my chest was from longing or sadness. I felt lost. Until that moment I had never felt that I belonged anywhere. I was a rootless tree. My gaze rose above the clouds and I remembered my childhood belief in God, who was swinging in a hammock, up there in Heaven. A brief smile brightened my face. I closed my eyes and prayed to God to show me the way, so I could find a good and honest job, and find some peace and joy in my life. Was that too much to ask?

The trip was uneventful, and when we landed at the Miami airport, everything seemed like a dream, especially for a first-timer like me. Until then, I had only made one journey in my life, when I moved from my hometown in the São Paulo countryside to the state capital.

We were cheerfully greeted by Sergio's friend, a Cuban national named Mario Hernandez, who took us straight to his home. Along the way, I noticed the beauty of the highway, the modern buildings, and the wide streets. It was as if we had reached the Promised Land.

Mario's house, which from then on would be our home too, was quite simple. It was located in a modest residential neighborhood, in the outskirts of the city.

Mario announced that we were going to Orlando the next day. We would leave very early in the morning, and would return at night. We would finally have the opportunity to visit the famous Disney World.

The next day, we woke up very early. My whole body was sore due to the hours of travel the day before. But my excitement was so great that I completely forgot about it. We took the car and headed to Orlando. The journey, for me, was full of surprises. I was enchanted by the beauty of the manicured gardens, the majestic buildings, the broad and clean streets, and the cheerful people driving their wonderful cars on the avenues, just like in the movies.

I felt that I was living in a dream, especially when we entered one of the most famous parks in the world, which until then I only knew from pictures. I concluded, at that moment, that the much-talked-about American dream was real, that it truly existed. We had an amazing day. For lunch, we ate the tastiest hot dog I had ever savored in my life, accompanied by lots of French fries, and a huge soda. For dessert, we had the biggest ice cream cone I had ever seen. It was just delicious.

We returned to Miami at the end of the day, exhausted

but happy. However, that carefree time being tourists would not last for long. We had to come back from the clouds and face reality. The next morning, we were introduced to the owner of a landscaping business, who seemed to be a very friendly person who would give us an opportunity to work.

His accent revealed that he had come from a Latin American country, probably Cuba. He later confirmed that was true. But as an American citizen already, he was willing to help newcomers.

So, that was how it all started, or rather, it started again, since I was once more facing heavy and hard work that I disliked, in a low-skilled job that did not utilize my college education. It was summer in Florida, and the high temperatures punished me with a blistering heat that I was not accustomed to, even though I was born in a tropical country.

The work began very early in the morning, always with the loading and unloading of tools. Each garden had its own peculiarities; each customer had distinctive needs and gave us different specifications. We had to be very careful, and follow exactly what had been agreed on with the company's owner. After pruning, and planting new seeds, we would clean the whole site. We stopped for a half-hour lunch, to eat a sandwich, drink a soda, and then continue to work until 6:00 or 7:00 p.m.

We returned home exhausted and with sunburned skin. Our dinner was usually very poor, a piece of pizza or any type of cheap processed food. For me, who had experienced hunger in the past, it was not so bad. At least we had something to eat.

I soon learned the correct use of gardening tools, and the work became easier, less complicated. I even got used to the heat, storms, insects, and my poor diet. What filled me with hope and courage, every day, was the possibility of living a new experience, being well paid, and learning new things, such as the customs and language of the American people.

I had a genuine admiration for the patriotism of Americans. I admired the way their houses often displayed their flag, the ultimate symbol of their country, with such pride and respect.

Learning the language was not only a matter of pride, but also of survival. I practiced my listening skills by watching television, and practiced my conversation skills by speaking with anyone I could find. Slowly, I started to master English.

Any time I had access to magazines or newspapers, sometimes found in the trash, I would read them carefully, seeking to learn the language as accurately as possible. I began to like English. Gradually, I also got used to living with Americans and other Latin Americans. I respected their customs, mindful that any misstep could lead to my deportation, since I only had a tourist visa, even though I was working.

It was not an easy adaptation, though. We missed our country, our former job, our friends, and, in Sergio's case, the family he left behind. Back then, the means of communication were considerably more limited than we have today. Several times, I saw tears fall from my friend's eyes.

As for myself, I had many doubts, and questioned whether I had done the right thing, leaving my job, my home, and the people I knew, to begin anew in a strange country. Could I get used to this new life?

Several months passed, and our tourist visas were expiring. Mario, who knew many people living in the country without a permanent residency, believed that applying for an extension would be too risky. However, we had no other process to get permission to live in the country legally. After five months in the United States, I started to rethink my stay in the country. I had never broken the laws of my homeland, and breaking laws in another nation clashed with my values as a lawyer.

But when I least expected it, I understood the wisdom of an old saying, "God writes straight with crooked lines." One morning, we went to perform our biweekly maintenance services for one of our customers. It was a very large house, almost a mansion. At the time of our arrival, the owner of the house was moving his car when he scratched it lightly on the mailbox post.

Getting out of the vehicle, he muttered to himself. "Oh look at that! I just bought it and this happens!"

I approached him and, after quickly examining the damage, I decided to talk to him, even with my less than fluent English.

"Don't worry. This paint on your car is from the mailbox post. Tomorrow is Saturday, and if you want, I can come here after my shift, and repair both the mailbox and your car. With a little wax and a good polishing your car will be like new. The body was not damaged, and I can assure you that there won't be a visible scratch."

He looked at me somewhat surprised, and a little suspicious. What could a gardener know about fixing cars? However, he accepted my offer, thanked me politely, and left.

I went there the next day, after an exhausting day of work, bringing some rags, a polishing paste and an automotive wax. I rang the bell and was greeted by a servant. I told her who I was, and a few minutes later the house's owner appeared at the door. He greeted me cordially, disguising his surprise at the fact that I had kept my promise and had returned. He asked my name and introduced himself. His name was John Adams. He was a tall, strong-looking American, about 60 years old.

I asked him if I could start the job and he agreed. There were four large vehicles in the garage, but I did not know their makes. Well, let's work, I thought. I started with the simplest task, and painted the mailbox post with spray paint. After that, I fixed the car's scratch. Luckily, it was actually very easy to do. I decided to polish the whole car. I was finishing when I saw him standing there, behind me.

He examined the car to see if the repair went well, turned to me and declared, a little surprised, "Good job!"

Then, he looked around and, seeing that the whole vehicle was waxed and shining, asked me how much I would charge him for the work.

I told him that, since he was a customer of the company, I would not charge him anything. It was a courtesy. He insisted, but I was adamant. Finally, he offered me something to drink, which I gladly accepted, because it was a very hot day, and I was sweating profusely.

He asked me to follow him into the house. I could not disguise my astonishment at the beauty and good taste of the decor, because until then I had only been in very modest houses, and had never imagined myself in a place like that. He led me to a pool, in the back, and introduced me to his wife, who was also very friendly. He then asked the servant to bring me juice or soda.

I did not sit down until I was invited. He was very courteous and unpretentious, which left me impressed.

We started a conversation, and after some time, he tactfully asked me where I was from, and why I was in the United States.

Briefly, I told him I was a lawyer in my homeland, but the opportunity to find a more rewarding salary had motivated me to change my life.

Mr. Adams commented, "A lawyer-turned-gardener, how interesting. Actually, I am a lawyer as well."

Our conversation, which could have lasted only a few minutes, just for the sake of politeness, went on for two hours. He asked me about life in my country, my hopes and dreams for my life in the United States, and so on.

I left Mr. Adams' house extremely impressed with his gracious and gentlemanly manners. Interestingly enough, it felt like we were old friends.

He followed me to the door, and told me he wanted to talk to me again about my training as a lawyer, which left me nervous and excited at the same time. I felt my face turn pale, but I nodded with a broad smile on my face.

CHAPTER 5

The Interview

A few days later, I received a phone call from a very pleasant woman, who introduced herself as Dorothy and told me that she was John Adams' secretary. She said that Mr. Adams would like to talk to me, and asked if she could schedule a meeting for us.

I was very surprised and intrigued, because I had believed that he was just being courteous and friendly to a professional colleague from another country when we had our conversation earlier. I asked myself, why not accept his invitation?

On the day of our meeting, I headed to the address I had been given, dressed in appropriate attire, a suit and a tie, borrowed from a colleague. From the entrance, I noticed that the building was very imposing. I must admit I felt intimidated when I realized that the office occupied several floors. But, as the saying goes, "If you cannot take the heat, get out of the kitchen." The only thing to do was to pull myself together and face the situation.

The receptionist told me where to go. I arrived on his floor and identified myself. A secretary received me politely, and soon after I was led to a huge conference room.

Who could have imagined?, I thought. A lawyer-turned-gardener, like me, being invited to a meeting in such a sophisticated place as this.

Mr. Adams entered the room, and greeted me cordially, seeking to put me at ease.

After some small talk, he explained that he was interested in my situation. He recognized my efforts, my determination and resourcefulness. He also praised my verbal fluency and advanced language skills, gained in spite of my limited contact with English speakers. According to him, that demonstrated an excellent capacity for learning outside the classroom. He believed he had an opportunity for me, since I was so dynamic and had such ambition. I could be useful to his law firm in the area of immigration law.

"I have a proposal for you, Francisco," he announced, and then asked me if I would like to work in his law firm as a paralegal. He told me that I would have to improve my English. But, since I would initially assist Brazilians and other Latin Americans, and considering that I spoke some

Spanish, it would not be much of a problem.

If I accepted his offer, someone from his staff would take on the task of regularizing my immigration status, doing what was necessary for me to start working as soon as possible. He also suggested I attend an intensive English program, paid for by the law firm.

I was stunned. I could not believe what I was hearing. It seemed that a gift from Heaven was being dropped into my lap.

In that moment, I thought back to my childhood again, remembering my friend Mr. Roberto and my father. Maybe they had talked with God, and the Lord of Life decided to give me this opportunity to finally fulfill my dreams, but in a way that I had never imagined.

I struggled to contain my tears, and to maintain my composure in front of this kind-hearted gentleman, who had so generously offered such a wonderful opportunity to an immigrant he barely knew, just a modest assistant gardener.

I exclaimed, "I have no words to thank you!"

Smiling, he replied, "If you don't have the words to thank me, then don't thank me." Still smiling, he added, "If you accept my offer, I'll ask my secretary to take you to our Human Resources Department, so they can oversee the details of your employment, salary, and so on."

I left the room overwhelmed, afraid I would collapse, since my legs were shaking, and my heart was thumping against my chest.

I followed the secretary to another floor, heading to the Human Resources Department, but more importantly, heading toward a new life, buoyed by the good wishes from Mr. Adams.

CHAPTER 6

A Friendly Conversation

"This is not going to work!"

That was the first thing I heard from Sergio when I returned to Mario's house, the generous friend who had so graciously welcomed us and gave us a place to live.

He explained, "You don't know anything about this country, you don't speak English very well, and you will be chewed up and spit out by other lawyers, because your training only matters in Brazil, not in the United States."

"But Sergio," I argued, "What have I got to lose? My life has always been filled with difficulties, hard work and sacrifices. Perhaps this is my chance to change things. If I don't try, I'll never know. If things don't work out, I'll grab whatever I have, which is next to nothing, and go back to Brazil, pronto! I'll take a chance, that's why I came to this country." Sergio lowered his head and replied, "Maybe you're right. What do you have to lose, right? Forgive my pessimism. I wish you the very best of luck and success."

Those words remained in my head. Luck? Well, if there really is such a thing as luck, I would need it dearly. However, I never believed in luck, I always thought that we make our own way, with a lot of determination, and always relying on God's blessings and love.

I arranged it with Mario so I could continue living in his house. Of course, I would keep paying rent, which I had been doing since I arrived in the country.

Mario was a simple man, and we had a lot in common. Like me, he had experienced many hardships, not only in his native Cuba, but also during his first years in the United States, which were very difficult. He had a tough time working and supporting his family.

He knew only too well the struggles faced by immigrants, who have to overcome language barriers and get used to an unfamiliar culture. Basically, moving to another country means dealing with a whole new and distinctive collective consciousness, which varies greatly from one nation to another.

In Cuba, many people discouraged him from immigrating to the United States, saying that Americans, for the most part, were cold people and only lived for themselves. I told him that in Brazil many people thought the same thing, at least the people I knew.

Mario, however, disagreed with that point of view. "You know, Francisco," he declared, "Ignorance is bliss. Yet, regarding the Americans, I think it's the other way around. I got to know them over the years, and found that they were respectful of other people's beliefs and way of life. I also discovered that they're a people of faith and capable of being caring and compassionate. Today I have many Americans friends, whom I care about, and they care about me."

"I agree with you," I replied. "Mr. Adams seemed to be a very generous person, especially towards me, a simple assistant gardener. I say that with all due respect to the profession of gardening, of course. But you understand me, no? I'm a foreigner in this country, and I hope I can, one day, overcome this mentality that makes us believe that we're second-class people. I'm not a defeatist, but I've talked with other immigrants, whom I've met in these past few months, and I realized that this mindset is very common, especially among the ones that aren't here legally. Several of them have good educations, including college degrees, but they didn't have any good opportunities in their countries, so they decided to change their lives. Now they suffer because they miss their families, because of the poor conditions under which they live, and because they don't have legal status in this nation. Their greatest desire is to contribute to this country because, as tough as their lives are here, it's still better than the lives they had in their homelands."

Mario answered. "I think exactly the same way, Francisco. I missed my homeland so much it hurt, but I needed to learn how to reinvent myself. I had to transform my immigrant self to an American self. It took a while, no doubt, for this change to become reality, but it happened. My life, while modest, is thriving. My children are growing up happily, and attending good schools. All in all, I realized that this is the land of opportunity for those who are willing to work hard. I'm now an American citizen, and this country gave me all I have, but most of all, it gave me dignity and recognition for my work ethic and effort. I really hope, Francisco, that you not only understand what I'm saying, but that you follow it. I'm aware that my experiences are the experiences of a simple man, but I've always strived to learn, and I've taken advantage of the opportunities that came my way, to make a better life for myself."

He concluded. "What I can say to you is, go ahead, because, as far as I'm concerned, you'll always have a friend with open arms. Seize this opportunity, and put all your energy in to it. This nation, and more importantly, God will support your desire to succeed and to contribute to this society which is opening its doors to you in the person of Mr. Adams." That night, I went to my bed with the distinct impression that the advice I had gotten was what I would have received from my father, if he had not passed away so soon, when I was still a little boy.

CHAPTER 7

The Beginning

The next morning, I went to the law firm carrying all the necessary documents, full of anxiety and expectation. I was fully aware that things would be difficult at first. I would have to work during the day, and take English classes in the evenings. Furthermore, I would have to familiarize myself with the American legal system, which is considerably different from the Brazilian system.

Every day, I brought home books and specialized articles, and studied them until late in the night. My weekends were more of the same. I was determined to succeed, so learning was the operative word for me. I studied not only the law, but also English grammar.

When my English skills started to improve, I asked Mario to teach me Spanish. Many of our clients were Latin Americans, and I could better assist them if I spoke their language correctly. It was not only a matter of politeness, but also a matter of respect.

Mario was very helpful, and told me, *"No te preocupes. Tranquilo que voy a enseñarte. ¿Para que son los amigos?"*[1]

It was one more challenge for me to overcome. As if there were not enough things for me to worry about. But this was my great opportunity, and I would not waste it. If there really was such thing as the American dream, I would turn it into reality.

The struggles I had to endure, from my childhood, were a great exercise in determination, and strengthened my will. Furthermore, I never dismissed God and Jesus from my existence, quite the contrary. I have always sought to live according to their divine plan, without any pretense, just doing the best I could.

It was the gospel of Jesus Christ that inspired me to seek a better life for myself. For that reason, I always kept in mind the old phrase, "God helps those who help themselves."

My work visa was requested by my law firm. It was usually a long and bureaucratic process, since it was a type of visa that the American government had little interest in granting. However, the approval came through promptly. I told Mr. Adams, when he called me to his office to give me the good news, "Thank you so have done for me, sir. With this visa, I can now become someone in life."

---

1 Don't worry. I'll teach you. That's what friends are for.

He gave me a great smile.

It was a first step, for sure. But I felt that the doors were starting to open for me, in all directions.

The days went by quickly, and I arranged an internship with one of the most experienced attorneys in the firm, so I could start my training.

My job was to make the first contact with a client, summarize the case, make suggestions, and then send the case to my colleagues, who had more knowledge about immigration law.

After some time, perhaps two months or so later, Mr. Greg, who was my mentor, informed me that I could start to work on my own. He considered me able and ready to perform my duties.

CHAPTER 8

Changes

My language skills improved considerably. My English was much better, and I managed to upgrade my rudimentary *portunhol*[2] to a passable Spanish. I realized that I had a knack for learning languages. One of my English teachers, a New Yorker, told me that he was impressed by how quickly I learned, and that my accent was very good.

After hearing about my situation, he decided to help me improve my pronunciation, correcting some nuances of the language, and softening my Brazilian accent, which was particularly heavy when I pronounced some words. Gradually, I started to be accepted in the community.

---

2 The word portunhol (in Portuguese) is a portmanteau of the words Português (Portuguese) and Espanhol (Spanish), and it is often given to the unsystematic and simplified mixture of the Portuguese and Spanish languages. It allows speakers of either Portuguese or Spanish, who are not proficient in the other language, to communicate with each other.

Americans did not appear to be the scary "bogeymen" that many people imagined. On the contrary, every day I realized that they were ethical and honorable, and that they valued the effort made by those who worked hard and sought to make a better life for themselves, thereby contributing to society as a whole.

With my teacher's support, who later became a very dear friend, as did his entire family, I felt motivated and accepted. I promised myself that I would make every effort to become an American citizen, and a respected lawyer, well-regarded by the community.

I needed to aim high, because I had lived in the margins of society for a very long time; long enough to learn that I needed to take full advantage of every opportunity I got. If the United States was the land of opportunities, I would not miss any. I had to keep the flame alive within myself, because I was well aware of the challenges that waited for me.

The first goal of my self-improvement plan was to move to another home, since I was still living in Mario's house, where I shared a room with Sergio. Mario, or the Cuban, which was how I started to call him after a joke we shared about his nationality, treated me well and respectfully. He and his wife became great friends, always seeking to fulfill my needs in the best way they could and as promptly as possible. They were really helping me to better myself and achieve my goals. But I needed to become more independent.

As for Sergio, it did not take long for him to tell us that he had given up on living in the United States. He had reached that decision despite my appeals and his conversations with the Cuban encouraging him not to give up, to persist a little longer.

"Maybe," I told him, "one day I can find a spot for you at the office. Of course, everything is very new, but who knows?"

A very dejected Sergio replied, "I have had enough, my friend. For me, the dream is over. I'm going back to Brazil, to resume my career. My life here is too tough. I won't get anywhere. What can I expect, being an assistant gardener? I'm done!"

I tried to argue, "But Sergio, you were the most enthusiastic and insisted so fervently that we come here. You knew the obstacles that waited for us, but that can change. This is a huge country, and it can offer new opportunities for you too."

"Nah! Every day, I feel more limited by stereotypes. Many people don't even greet me. It's like I don't exist! They see me as a mere employee, a lawn mower. If I keep going this way, soon I'll not just cut grass, but I'll eat grass too. I feel like I'm becoming a brute. I feel like I have no value."

"At least, in my country, I can walk around freely, and live as a citizen. My visa will expire soon, and then I'll live like a criminal, risking deportation at any time. What will I achieve by that? Experience? I'm tired of living like a loser!"

When I tried to argue once again, he became aggressive and said harshly, "Sorry, Francisco, but you lived like a 'nobody' your whole life. You had to overcome many adversities, and maybe that gave you an iron will which I don't have. What can I do if I'm not like that?"

His words did not offend me, but they immediately triggered many painful memories. I felt like a knife was being shoved in to my heart. In fact, I had been a "nobody" for much of my life, but my friend did not have to be so cutting in his remarks.

Since my childhood, life had always been arduous, beginning with the children who avoided me because of my poverty, something that I only understood much later. Today I know that their mothers were probably afraid that I would infect them with some kind of disease. What a joke! As if poverty is contagious! It is not contagious. What sickens the soul is prejudice. I knew that only too well.

For a long time, I had been a target of prejudice which is a true cancer of society. It pitilessly consumes people's hearts who, because of their pride and ignorance, insist on nurturing it, not making any effort to root it out.

I did not let those bitter feelings overwhelm me. With great difficulty, I hid the tears filling my eyes. My friend was unburdening himself, and I felt I should support him.

"I can only say, Sergio, that our friendship will continue, and I wish you all the success in the world. If I can improve my life here, I promise I'll visit you in Brazil, and one day, if I get a place of my own, I would love to have you as my guest."

Hiding my sadness, I decided to go for a walk, hoping some fresh air might help me clear my head.

CHAPTER 9

Starting My New Job

The challenges surfaced early in my work as a paralegal. Never was I so tested in my patience and self-control, as when I had my first client interview. The interview was with a Brazilian woman named Cláudia S.

When she arrived, I noticed that she was a strikingly beautiful woman in her early thirties. She was a brunette, with expressive green eyes, and a tanned and well-defined body, probably sculpted in long hours of physical activity. She certainly knew how to highlight her beauty by tastefully wearing expensive clothes.

I greeted her and introduced myself, in a friendly and polite manner which was not reciprocated. I had the impression that she looked down at me with disdain. Perhaps she expected someone older, more experienced, like the president of our law firm. Her abrupt questions proved me right.

"What is your position at this law firm? Sorry, I forgot your name."

"Francisco Martins."

"Oh, yes, Mr. Martins, I have an important matter to resolve, but I don't think you have enough experience to deal with it."

I thought she was arrogant and disrespectful, questioning me in such a rash and rude manner. However, I answered very politely.

"Ms. S., I understand your concern, but I can assure you I am able to conduct your first interview. This is my job. However, if necessary, your case will be referred to another professional."

With an air of displeasure, she went straight to the point. "I need your law firm to draft a contract, as I intend to hire the services of an American."

I did not quite understand, at first, what her intentions were. So I asked, in a casual manner, "Contract? Are you aware that our law firm deals specifically with immigration matters? What type of contract are you talking about?"

She made a haughty expression, looked at me in a condescending manner and explained, "I'm arranging a marriage with an American citizen, in order to legalize my situation here in the United States, and get my green card. This method is much faster and easier than any other. I'll pay fifteen thousand dollars to this American, in two installments of seven thousand five hundred dollars. The first installment will be paid on the wedding day, and the second when my documentation is ready. I don't want to be surprised with a last minute withdrawal. Therefore, to protect my investment, I need a contract including some guarantees."

I was taken aback. It was my first case, and I had someone in front of me who was seeking to do something completely illegal, and was speaking about it very casually, as if describing something trivial like the purchase of new clothes. It was astounding. Not satisfied with just an arranged marriage, she wanted to compound her wrongdoing by writing a contract that would formalize her fraud, giving her some sort of guarantee that the "service" would be provided. It was error upon error.

At first, I remained expressionless, not showing any reaction, as if I had not heard such nonsense. Obviously, I knew very well that countless immigrants used those schemes to obtain their legal residency. Desperately, they sought to legalize their status by any means, in order to remain in the country where they chose to live. However, I was completely opposed to this type of arrangement. Furthermore, it was against the law firm's policy and principles to be involved with any kind of illegality.

I remembered, at that moment, a conversation I had about the ethics of our law firm, with one of the most experienced attorneys in the company who was helping me in my training. Firmly, he told me, "In case of doubt about the legality of any case, we prefer to give it up immediately. Before all else, we have a name to protect."

I agreed with that policy wholeheartedly. I never found it acceptable for a lawyer to employ shady means to promote his or her interests, or those of a client. It would be akin to a physician who, seeking financial compensation, prescribed a surgery he or she knew would be contraindicated or harmful to the patient.

I was a relatively well-informed person, and had a modicum of common sense, enough to know that inappropriate situations can occur in any field or in any profession, but I have always opposed the follow-like-sheep mentality, and rejected the lame rationalization that "Everyone does it."

I would rather preserve my integrity, even after hearing people state that in my profession I could choose either to be an ethical and poor lawyer, or an unethical but very rich one.

I was praised by some who held the principles of my profession in high regard. Others, whose values were questionable and who could be bought with any sum of money, considered me a fool. I preferred to be called a fool, because my conscience was clear, knowing that I always sought to do my best, in the most open, transparent way possible.

I would never willingly employ illicit means to succeed in life, or to enjoy any position or situation that was not achieved with morality, dignity and honesty. I came from a very impoverished background, but learned very well that the rejecting of life's core values is one of the most insidious diseases, because it kills the character. Apart from that, poverty is not necessarily as fatal as many people believe. Being poor is not the worst thing that can happen to a person. Lack of character, on the other hand, is the absolute poverty of the soul.

I am not self-righteous, and I never possessed moralistic intentions to become so, but I always believed that being an ethical person is essential because my honest behavior could have a positive impact on those around me, thereby benefiting society as a whole.

Because I was looking a little more concerned, trying to think of an adequate response, the client asked impatiently, "Well, aren't you going to say anything?"

"Ms. S.," I explained calmly, "Unfortunately, our office does not handle such matters. But, if you allow me, I will give you my advice for your situation. I strongly suggest that you do not enter into this type of marriage because it is completely illegal. Even worse, to sign a contract for such a marriage would actually formalize the fraud, and may bring grievous consequences for you."

She got very upset, her expression showing anger and disgust. Breaking the rules of civility, she exclaimed rudely, "Can you call your superior? You don't seem to have the experience or expertise for this type of transaction. Please call your boss, because I believe he'll resolve this."

I argued calmly, "Ms. S., I don't need to ask for my boss to intervene, because I know the ethics of my law firm very well, and nothing else can be done, other than what I'm already doing."

The beauty turned into a beast. She glared at me with her lovely green eyes, which at that moment were bloodshot. Scornfully, she shouted, with a now shrill voice, "Listen here, you little 'Mr. Nobody,' I didn't come here to waste my time, or to listen to your foolish speech about ethics. For you lawyers, ethics have a price tag. I know very well that it's only a matter of negotiation, so do what I'm asking you. Go call your boss!"

Once again, I was facing prejudicial and disrespectful treatment. She was insulting me, both on a personal and a professional level. To be called "Mr. Nobody"! The title

'Mister' was perfectly fine, of course; the problem was with that epithet, "Nobody", which I really could not stomach.

I took a deep breath, and tried to keep my self-control. It was my first client interview, and I would not embarrass myself. I was determined to handle the situation with poise and professionalism. I breathed deeply again, counted to three, and in a low, even voice, I told her, "Please, calm down."

"Don't tell me to calm down! I didn't come here looking for a speech, but for a solution to my problem."

"It's not a speech, but the right advice for your case. Neither I, nor any other professional in this office, will be able to assist you. Drafting the type of contract you want is completely out of the question."

She got up, and I thought she would attack me physically, since she had already tried attacking me emotionally. But I had to take care of my job, needed to preserve this great opportunity. So, I went to her and said, "I'll accompany you to the door."

Why did I say that?

Her cheeks were flushed, and her harsh words hit me like slaps.

"Listen to me, brat, you're just an errand boy. I don't need your courtesy, and I don't need your law firm. I know how to take care of myself. Go to hell!"

I realized at that moment that I was a master of 'turning the other cheek' because despite wanting to throttle her, I stopped myself and declared solemnly, "Farewell, Ms. S."

It did not take long for my boss to come into the room. He asked, smiling, "So, how was your baptism by fire? Was it successful? Did you enjoy it?"

"Not really," I answered. "Did you hear?"

"I did. I don't speak Portuguese, but I could tell that her temper was raging."

"Indeed. She wanted to legally formalize her absolutely illegal scheme. When I denied her, she went crazy. I'll ask the secretary to find me an aspirin, because that's what I need right now."

He smiled again and said, "We have a whole bottle for cases like that, and I suggest you buy some too, because from now on you'll sorely need them."

"Terrific. After the beating I just took, your words are so encouraging that I want to jump from the window," I replied jokingly.

He laughed with pleasure at my half-hearted, annoyed smile.

CHAPTER 10

Moving On

A t the end of the day, I went to my English language course which, modesty aside, was going very well. While I was on the bus, I started to reflect about anxiety, and how it can make people sick.

It was soon after my tumultuous meeting with Claudia S., and I was thinking about her case. It was a typical life situation for millions of people. Because they could not wait for life to present the right solution, at the right moment, they would go ahead and make a complete mess of the situation. They did not understand that patience is not practiced by sitting down and waiting passively; on the contrary, it involves working and doing their best, and waiting for the rewards of their effort to materialize, when the time is right.

It is like a fruit hanging from a tree needing time to mature. Day after day, impatience makes people sick, in mind and body. Some people even rely on chemicals to find some balance in their lives, or to ameliorate their suffering and calm the sense of panic they had created for themselves. Often, they tragically became dependent on those substances, leading some to rashly give up their lives with thoughtless actions because they were so exhausted by the stressful conditions they had unconsciously imposed upon themselves.

Also unconsciously, they are unduly influenced by other people's thinking and behavior. They feel an intense need to be like everybody else, ignoring the fact that human beings are unique. They confuse similarity to sameness, as if people were machines produced in a factory.

Such suffering we create for ourselves! I thought. Claudia S. was a typical example. She was quickly digging her own grave, shortening her life, by not controlling her thoughts, and therefore her actions.

At that moment, I realized that the whole scenario was a great lesson for me. I needed my job, but I also needed to utilize the wisdom that life was offering me.

Attending law school, for a second time, was one of my dreams and goals. Then, after graduating, I wanted to take the bar exam which would allow me to practice law in the United States; it was a similar process to the Brazilian bar exam which I had taken already. I was just starting out, but was already aiming to go further. As such, I did not want to waste my time with trivialities, whatever they might be. I was living in the land of opportunities, and my visa status was legal. There was no way that I would allow myself to miss that chance.

When I reached my destination, I put my thoughts aside, and went to my class focused on learning as much as I could. Later on, I got back to my Cuban friend's house, where I still lived. I needed to rest, because tomorrow I would have a hard day of work.

Most of my time in the office was dedicated to assisting senior attorneys, which was a rather bureaucratic, but also a highly stressful, job. Conducting client interviews was a part of my daily work, but I interviewed only one client per day. That was because I was still in training and my supervisor believed that I should gradually solidify my knowledge before I took on more client responsibilities. Immigration, he explained, was very complex legal field, and at the same time very rigorous, sometimes bordering on the extreme.

On a rainy afternoon, I was scheduled to interview a client named José R. to conduct the first evaluation of his case.

He seemed like a gift to me after going through that hurricane called "Claudia S." José was a young man, 28 years old like myself, and yet, he carried himself with the refined posture of a gentleman, and had a grave demeanor which made him look much older.

He greeted me politely, introducing himself as an employee of one of our client companies. He was transferred from the Brazilian subsidiary to take a position at the company's headquarters in Miami, a promotion that he had sought for four years.

He told me that he was very satisfied with the position and that he was confident he would meet their expectations. He considered himself very well prepared with substantial knowledge relevant to his work. Furthermore, he was fluent in English and Spanish, which he believed would help him advance his career.

He had gathered all the necessary documents to apply for a work permit, following the directions from his company's legal department. Then he came to us to deliver those documents, to start the 'Immigration Services' proceedings. However, he did not have the countenance of a happy person. His problem, if we could call it a problem, was that his fiancée refused to join him.

She worked for a large organization, and her career was thriving. As such, she "would not throw it all away," according to her own words, to follow him to the United States.

Thinking this was a simple, insignificant matter, I made some trivial encouraging remarks. But suddenly, I saw the tears in his eyes.

I tried to empathize, considering all the ways that some situations can be difficult and complicated. It was if he had won the lottery, but could not collect the prize. José had achieved an important position in his profession, which had required a great personal investment, as well as a strong commitment to his education and training. His new job gave him a boost in his career, in his salary, and gave him the chance to live in another country. Certainly, many people would trade places with him. But what about his personal feelings? How does one safely navigate through the affairs of the heart?

Of course, we do not always get what we want. It would be preposterous for anyone to think so. Yet, when it comes to romantic matters, we are often immature and unprepared, at a loss on how to deal with them.

One thing is undeniable, I learned. Immigrants, at least many of them, struggle to deal with their painful separation from family, loved ones, friends, homeland, and so on.

We are well aware that material things do not entirely fulfill our lives. Unfortunately, the high suicide rates in more developed countries prove that owning material goods is not enough to satisfy the longings of the heart, or to help us cope with our feelings.

We are much more than simple machines created to please ourselves or society. We are complex human beings, and we need the nourishment of love, which crowns our achievements in every other part of our lives.

What is the point of having light, if it is hidden and does not illuminate? What is the value of wealth, if we do not feel the joy of living?

I needed to say something to my client. I realized, at that moment, and facing that situation, that I should assume the role of a therapist of sorts, or a friend. I could not simply act as a legal counsel and ignore my client's emotional difficulties.

Actually, I never thought that my profession would excuse me from expressing my feelings. Even after dealing with very harsh people, some so tough and ruthless they resembled slave-drivers, I still believed that we cannot separate legal matters from emotions. After all, I was dealing with people, human beings.

I talked to him in a mild voice to help him think clearly and control his feelings. "José, I think this is just a phase you have to go through. Life always provides the right solutions to those who keep their focus on the good things and on their positive achievements. Above all, life provides the right solutions to those who seek the best for themselves, and for others, who help their families, and their community."

I added, "Perhaps your bride could also get a transfer one day, who knows?"

"Mr. Martins," he answered in a choked voice, "loneliness hurts, and cannot be filled with achievements. Three weeks here in the United States were enough to make me realize that this won't be easy."

"Relax, José! You just arrived!" I resisted the temptation to tell him part of my story, how the loneliness and abandonment I had to go through taught me some very important and unforgettable lessons. But I concluded that it would not be wise to talk about myself, because he might think I was trying to compete and that would not be appropriate.

I tried to cheer him up, saying that he would soon form a group of friends who would help him adapt to his new life in the country. Basically, I explained to him that he could lead a fairly normal life. Besides, he could visit his family and his fiancée in Brazil, and they could come and visit him, I argued.

When he left, he seemed more resigned. He thanked me profusely, not only for the legal assistance I provided, but also for the words of encouragement.

His visa was soon approved, since everything was in

order. I was happy for him. We were both young, but he was much better prepared. He came from a stable family and with an excellent education. Undoubtedly, he would rapidly rise to the top, and gain a prominent position at his company.

But, alas, that was not to be. As the old saying goes, "He who looks at the face does not see the heart."

I called José, to give him the news of his visa approval, but he was not very enthusiastic. However, I did not ask him anything, because in my position, I should not be meddling in the private lives of our clients. Anyway, I had done my part.

Time passed with my hectic schedule in the office, and I did not hear from José again, until I met him by chance on the streets of Miami. I had accepted an invitation from a coworker to go out for lunch. Such occasions were rare, since I always devoted my lunch time to studying legal cases and to practice English and Spanish; I seldom left the office.

I noticed a man in front of me, deep in thought, and then I realized it was José. I decided to approach him.

"Hello, José. How are you?"

He recognized me and answered, dejectedly, "I'm doing well, mostly."

I noticed that he seemed very distressed, but I continued

to chat with him, trying to inject some liveliness into the conversation.

"So, how are things going? Are you doing well in your new job? Are you adjusting?"

But he evaded my questions, telling me that he had an appointment and had to leave. He promised to call me later so we could talk some more.

I found the whole encounter a bit strange. I had expected him to have a very comfortable situation, especially compared to mine. But I did not insist, and waited for him to call me, since that was what he wanted.

I cannot explain it, but I always have been very sensitive, especially towards other people. I can sense when they are in trouble, as if the air around them announced it. I had read about the energetic emanations surrounding human beings, more commonly known as "auras," but never gave much importance to that kind of subject.

A few days later, I received a phone call from José. I was surprised, because I had not expected him to call me, despite his promise.

He greeted me politely and said, "Mr. Martins, I apologize for taking your time, but there are not many people I can talk to about this. I think you're the right person, since you don't work with me. I wonder if you could meet me, because I need help. I'm desperate."

I was surprised. I barely knew him. What type of help could he need from me? "What can I do for you, José?" I asked.

"I'd rather talk to you in person, outside of the office. I think you can at least listen to me, don't you?"

I could tell that he was anxious, so I did not keep him on the phone. We arranged to meet at a coffee shop near his office, even though I would have little time, since I had to attend class soon thereafter.

We met, and when I greeted him, I saw that he looked despondent. We shook hands, and I noticed that his hand was a bit cold and shaky.

After sitting down, I asked him, "Would you like some coffee, or anything else?"

"No, thank you. I know you don't have much time, and I'd like you to hear me out, because I don't have anyone to talk to. My friends from work are very busy, and might think I am only seeking attention. I don't want to look weak."

I felt even more intrigued. After all, what problem might he have that was so complicated?

He continued. "You remember when I told you I was engaged?"

"Yes, I remember."

"Well, it didn't take long for my fiancée to end our engagement, claiming that it'd be too difficult to maintain a long-distance relationship. She said she'd like to keep her focus on her career, and made it clear that she has no intention of leaving the country. She claimed that she was doing well in her job, and there was no way she'd drop everything to face a life of uncertainty in the United States. Despite all my pleas to wait for me to return to Brazil so we could talk in person, because I loved her, she didn't seem to care and callously hung up on me. But the worst was yet to come. After that, I heard from one of my friends that she was spotted kissing and hugging one of her coworkers. I don't know how I survived that, how my heart continued beating, not only because of that terrible news, but because of everything. I then lost my will to stay in Miami, to work, and even to continue living."

He added that life had lost all meaning, and that it would be a waste of time to pursue his goals.

At that point in our conversation, José's eyes had become red, and tears fell down his face. I realized that he was not nearly as strong as I had believed he was. Despite seeming very energetic, and being well-prepared intellectually, he had little control over his emotions. Still, it had all happened very recently, so I thought that in a few days he would recover his equilibrium, at least in part.

"José," I argued, "Eventually, you'll find another person who truly deserves your affection, respect and love. You've just arrived, and so far you've been doing very well. Relax, go see a doctor, perhaps a psychologist, but don't give up."

Unhappily, he replied, "I came here by overcoming many challenges, and fighting tooth and nail to get this position at my company. I left my friends, the comfort of my home, the affection of my family, and more importantly, I left my fiancée. I did all that to progress in my career, to achieve success in the shortest possible time, because my main goal was to marry Carmen, the woman I love, who left me at the first opportunity. She ran into someone else's arms as soon as she could. She lied to me, saying only that the distance between us was too great, and it'd take a long time for us to meet again."

"Of course you have every reason to be angry, depressed and very sad, but don't forget that life goes on. With your talent and training, you'll get out of this tough situation as a much stronger person. José, have you tried praying, to God, to Jesus, asking for the strength to overcome this trial? We're God's children, and He doesn't abandon us in our time of need. Try asking Him for strength."

"Oh, I don't know, Mr. Martins. I don't usually pray, and I have doubts about God's existence."

"Well, José, you have the right to doubt God's existence. However, it's when we are in pain that we realize how much we need Him. Because, unfortunately, it's in times of suffering that we discover we need to give our anguish over to the hands of the Lord, this divine force that knows and sustains us. Why don't you try talking to Him?"

I added, "The logic of life proves that things were not made randomly. God is so good, He doesn't even have to force us to believe in Him, isn't that so?"

He wiped his tears in the handkerchief I offered him, and told me, "I really appreciate you coming here and listening to me. Everything here is so strange to me, the environment, people who only think about themselves. No one cares. Now I really know the true meaning of loneliness."

I decided not to argue. He had a point, at least in part. However, what José was not taking into account was that by moving to another country, with different customs and traditions, he had made a change in his life. This change also represented an opportunity to immerse oneself in another culture. At least that was how I saw things. But this was not the time for a debate.

I spoke some more words of encouragement, and made myself available for anything he needed, not only as a professional, but also as a new friend, on whom he could rely.

He got up to leave, only saying to me, "Goodbye."

I watched his figure as he walked away, a little downcast,

only turning for a brief moment to wave goodbye with his hand.

That same night, José took his own life, by swallowing a huge dose of tranquilizers.

CHAPTER 11

Some Thoughts

I cannot deny that José's death shook me, even though I hardly knew him. I was deeply shocked.

Working in a law firm specializing in immigration cases, I started to understand, in essence, the struggles that immigrants have to go through, even those who could bring their families with them. It is an incredibly difficult process.

Their issues are far more complex than just overcoming language barriers, or learning new customs, or for some, even getting used to different types of food. Basically, immigrants have to undergo a challenging adaptation process into the new country's collective consciousness. By and large, they have to make a mighty effort to get included in a society that repeatedly denied them the right to do so, even if they were qualified.

Through my Cuban friend Mario, I had met many

people who were highly-qualified professionals in their homelands, including college graduates, teachers, managers, lawyers, and other such professionals. In the United States, however, they had to perform menial activities, such as cleaning, gardening, or working in the construction business. The problem was not that they had to work in those types of jobs, since I too had worked as an assistant gardener, cleaning patios and cutting grass. The problem was how they were perceived and treated.

Many times I had the misfortune of witnessing the contempt some people showed towards immigrants. Of course, it didn't always occur, but it happened more often than it should. One day, I noticed a girl about fifteen years old. Her mother was one of the Cuban's clients. The girl got home from school, and scolded her mother because she was talking with him in Spanish.

She declared, "Mom, you must speak English, because we're in our country, and this is our language. If these people are unable to speak English, it's their problem. Either they find a way to learn our language, or they should go back to where they come from."

Even though the girl's mother was born in the United States, she descended from Peruvians, and learned Spanish at home, from her parents.

Obviously, that type of opinion or attitude was not

shared by everyone. I have met, and still know, many Americans who are respectful and polite. In fact, the vast majority of them are like that.

However, some people look down upon immigrants, perhaps because they see them as invaders. For that reason, they seek to deport them by any means possible. With profound disrespect, those people disregard the human side of the issue, and do not take into account that each case is unique. Thus, they separate children from their parents, and treat immigrants like criminals. They forget that the immigrant, first and foremost, is a human being, and as such, deserves humane treatment.

No society on our planet can live in complete isolation. The ones that tried suffered the pains of extinction. We are sociable beings, children of God, and as such, brothers and sisters.

Besides the moral aspects, there are also economic and financial interests involved in the matter. Anyway, it would be wonderful if immigration officials adopted a more humane approach when dealing with those thorny issues.

I am a lawyer, and therefore I cannot conceive living in a world without laws and rules to govern our society. But to place everyone in the same level of illegality, as if they are all cut from the same cloth, is unfair, to say the least.

We often hear that immigrants who are in the country

illegally are unable to succeed in their homelands. This is a misguided notion. The vast majority are workers, seeking better opportunities and better living conditions. They are people who perhaps did not have many chances where they came from. It certainly was not because they did not try hard enough. Usually, the economy in their countries is underdeveloped, or the job market could not absorb all the professionals.

I sincerely doubt that an engineer, a lawyer, a dentist, or any other skilled worker, would not enjoy making a living from their chosen professions in their country of origin.

If there is a change, it is because life demands it. For that reason, people must be respected, not thought of simply as a number or a hindrance. We ought to remember that Christ himself taught us to love one another. Love has no borders, ethnicity, creed, and so on. Only he who does not love takes into account those differences, or rather, is indifferent, especially towards the pain of others.

It was clear to me that José's case was an example of the heartbreaking woes that afflict immigrants. But I would not let this problem go unanswered. I could not do much, but I would talk about it, and maybe I would create a network of solidarity. I would strive to raise awareness about the reality of immigrants, and help them get more support.

Loneliness, abandonment, and neglect hurt. It is not

a pain that a physician can cure, because it is rooted in the depths of a person. It is in the soul. There is only one remedy for that: respect.

Always Learning

T ime goes on, but as Humberto de Campos, a Brazilian writer who died in 1934, once wrote, "Time is God's medicine."

I completed my English course. I took the Test of English as a Foreign Language, or TOEFL, and achieved a very good score, which allowed me to enroll in law school. I was able to demonstrate, through my diploma and transcripts, that I had already obtained a degree in Brazil. Thus, I would be able to obtain my law degree in two years. In parallel, I started studying and preparing myself for the bar exam, because I had no intention of wasting any time. I was fluent in Spanish as well.

I was totally focused on finishing law school and passing the bar exam, which would allow me to actually practice law, and upgrade my position within the firm. I had a respectable job as a paralegal, which was similar to an intern or a legal assistant. But I did not want to be a paralegal forever. I wanted to grow and achieve stability. I was fully convinced that I could do it.

But until that happened, I was still responsible for most of the bureaucratic tasks at our office. I had to perform the typical duties of a legal intern, and do the things that most people avoided doing. Furthermore, on some occasions, I still had to bring coffee or lunch to my more qualified coworkers, like an office-boy, a job I had done when I was fifteen years old. Although those types of things were not part of my duties, and took valuable time, I did it without any resentment. I was grateful to those people who were helping me learn and get acquainted with the law, court rules and procedures, and were teaching me how to prepare and solve legal matters. I was building a solid body of knowledge, and making friendships. Kindness generates kindness.

I realized that I was getting popular among my coworkers when invitations to barbecues, or to watch basketball games, began to come more often.

Before long, I started to be entrusted with more delicate and complex immigration matters, such as the case of a homosexual couple who wanted to apply for work permits. Maria and Lucia, as they were called, were Latin Americans, and had been living in the United States for a little more than a month.

Lucia was the more assertive one, and took the lead in our conversation explaining their situation in a fast-paced Spanish.

"We came here because of the prejudice that exists in our country against homosexuality. While we lead a discreet life, we face many difficulties in our jobs, and even in our social life. Most of the towns in our country are very small, which pretty much means that everyone knows everyone. Unfortunately, there is a great bias against gays in our culture. We've heard from friends and acquaintances who immigrated to the United States that we're much more respected and accepted over here. We try not to draw attention, avoiding any show of affection in public, because we don't want to offend anyone. We just want to live a normal life, and enjoy the respect we deserve. Well, we need a work permit, so we can remain here without any problem."

"I understand your situation perfectly, and I find it quite natural that you want to remain here, under the circumstances. However, we need to analyze your case carefully. I know that you want to apply for a work permit, but how did you get into the country?"

"We entered as tourists, but we have no intention of going back."

"I understand, but I must explain to you how the work

permit works, because the immigration law for a work permit involves a number of issues and requirements that have to be met."

"If your request for a work permit is not granted, the alternative is to live here illegally. You know that, right? In my view, this is your worst possible option, because you'll have to hide from the immigration services, and live under the constant threat of deportation. If this happens, you may have no other choice but to go back to your country. You'll face prejudice, but you would also live under a legal status."

Lucia seemed very upset. She looked at Maria, making faces, and demonstrating her outrage.

She then angrily retorted. "What part of everything I just said didn't you understand? Maybe I was not clear enough. You heard when I say that we don't want to go back? We're here so that you can do something about that. We decided to pay for your services so that you could arrange a permanent visa for us, because we won't return to our country."

I thought to myself, oh boy, it is going to be one of those days.

I told her. "Yes, I heard and understood you perfectly. But applying for a work permit is not so simple. You came here as a tourist, and now you want a work permit. That's not how immigration works. You cannot enter into the country as a tourist, and become a permanent resident, just like that, because that's what you want. The authorities will not just accept your desire to move here. There are legal requirements governing the process that must be fulfilled."

She took a deep breath and replied, "In other words, you're telling me that there is nothing you can do?"

"I'm not using 'other words' at all. I'm telling you very clearly that there is nothing we can do for you. There is a huge amount of regulation imposed by the American government on the immigration process. It's not enough to want to immigrate, you must meet a number of prerequisites, and unfortunately, from what I could see in your case, you don't fulfill them. Basically, you don't meet the eligibility criteria for any kind of permanent visa available."

Lucia's reaction was completely unexpected. She got up and angrily started insulting me. "You're a bigot and a cheap sleazebag. You think you'll get the money for this consultation without doing anything?"

"Please calm down. First, I'm not a bigot. Second, the fee for this legal consultation doesn't belong to me, but to this law firm."

"I want my money back, and I want it now. Indeed, I was told that lawyers in the United States are a bunch of crooks, who only think about taking people's money without doing anything for them. You're just a thug and a thief like the others."

She was shouting, in a scene worthy of a melodrama. The screams caught the attention of other employees.

However, this deplorable episode taught me that we are sorely wrong when we think that things are so bad they cannot get any worse, because they certainly can.

A coworker quickly entered the room, asking in English if I wanted to call security.

The situation then got much more serious, because Lucia understood what was happening, and resorted to physical violence. First, she picked up a wooden desk tray for incoming paperwork, and with quick precise movements hurled it at my colleague, hitting him squarely in the chest.

Maria desperately tried to control her partner, but without success. Lucia then lunged at me, screaming swear words that I had never heard before. She grabbed the phone from my desk, and holding it like a knife, tried to bang my head with it.

She put half the office in an uproar. Several colleagues came to help. One called the police, while another went to find a security guard. A third grabbed her by the waist, trying to control the situation.

Kicking and screaming, Lucia tried to use her nails to hurt his face. She wildly kicked everything and everyone who tried to approach her.

The security guards finally came, and had trouble containing her. They dragged her out of the office, while she screamed that she would come back and kill me.

"I'll wait for you in the street, and when you leave here, I'll kill you, you second-rate lawyer! Scumbag!"

The situation got even worse when the police arrived. They had to use pepper spray in her eyes to subdue her. It seemed that the fracas would never end. It was amazing— the amount of strength and energy that she had. Finally, they handcuffed her and took her to the police station.

Maria was very distraught. Crying and shaking, she looked like she was on the verge of a breakdown. Someone gave her water with sugar, and she gradually calmed down.

The hurricane was finally over, and things quieted down. Mr. Adams, who heard the pandemonium from his office, sent a lawyer to the police station, to see what could be done, while I wondered if I would get fired after that scene.

But after the storm comes the calm. The calm arrived, thank God, through Maria's words.

"I'm so sorry. Lucia is always like that when she loses her control. Forgive this whole mess, but she's been without her medication for days now. She can't buy it here, because she needs a prescription for that. I insisted that she go see a doctor and not stop her treatment."

She spoke in Spanish. Another colleague translated her words to Mr. Adams, to avoid any conflict of interest, since my conduct was under review.

This angel, savior of my hide, continued, "This guy," she said referring to me, "was only giving us legal advice, but she has very rigid views on certain things, and sees bigotry in everything."

She once again apologized, and went to the police station to see her partner.

Mr. Adams waited for things to quiet down, and told me, "Come talk to me later, ok?"

I just nodded affirmatively.

CHAPTER 13

Unexpected News

It was already 6:00 p.m. when I went to Mr. Adams' office. As always, he received me with his calm gaze and his gentle manner of speaking.

I was ready for the worst. After the debacle with Lucia, I fully expected to be fired.

He greeted me cordially, and asked, "How are things going? Or as they say in Brazil," and he spoke in the best Portuguese he could muster, "*Tudo bem?*"[3]

"I could be better, you know. Messy incidents, like the one today, shake anyone."

"Those things happen, Francisco. We are not just attorneys. Sometimes, or perhaps most of the time, we're also psychologists, counselors, friends, and in the opinion of those whom we cannot be of any assistance, villains."

I was puzzled. I was certain I would be fired, but the

---

3 Is everything OK?

conversation was taking another turn.

"I understand," I replied, "but it's never easy to manage situations that are completely beyond our control. Believe me, I tried the best I could. If I made any mistake, it was being too honest and straightforward with the client. She thought that immigration is merely a matter of will, that it was the same thing as asking for a hot dog in a snack bar."

"It's the lack of information that creates this type of misconception. Some people, not all of them, have no idea how these matters work. When you try to explain the situation to them, they don't make any effort to understand it, or classify us as incompetent, as if we are all cut from the same cloth."

Mr. Adams spoke, "But I didn't call you here to talk about that poor woman's case. Soon after the disturbance, I asked Mr. Rick to go to the police station, and see what could be done. He dealt with the matter in the best way he could. Even the police officers could see that it was a case of illness. Then, Maria arrived and told them about her partner's lack of medication, and things were pretty much resolved. Later, you can speak to whoever has more information about the case and ask what happened. Don't worry."

"I shouldn't worry? But she told me she would come back and kill me."

He laughed easily, and countered, "If everyone who threatened to kill us carried out his or her intent, we lawyers would need nine lives, like cats! In any case, Francisco, while you're still alive, tell me, how is your work, and your life?"

"I'm learning a lot in my work. Besides the bureaucratic part, I've seen a few cases that are truly interesting. The crown jewels, so to speak. Furthermore, I finished my English course, and as you've heard, I got an excellent score on my TOEFL exam."

"Yes, I've heard about that. Congratulations!"

"Thank you. I've been practicing my Spanish with my Cuban friend. I've read and written a lot in this language, and I believe I'm doing well."

"This is all great. I believe that you should keep focused on your goals. Now that you're fluent in English, you should enroll in a law school, and then prepare yourself to take the bar exam, and become a licensed lawyer. Are you still studying?"

"Yes!"

"Excellent! Francisco, you've been an inspiration to many people here in the firm. Your dedication and commitment are admirable. Messy situations like today aren't the norm, but they happen. The important thing is that you don't get discouraged, and that you remain focused on your goals."

He continued. "I look at you, and I remember the beginning of my career. I also had to work very hard. Today, I don't know if I'd have the strength to do it again. It was normal, back then, to sleep little, eat poorly, and live only to work and to study. But nothing is achieved in life without hard work and dedication, isn't that so?"

For someone who thought that his job was hanging by a thread, this was a huge and welcome surprise. I was getting a real infusion of encouragement and understanding.

In life, unfortunately, there are few people who are genuinely happy with the achievements and felicities of others. Envy, on the other hand, frequently derails those who want to do something for themselves, or their community.

Sadly, there are those who see our grit and determination, and seek to put us down, and they may end up discouraging us. But if we keep our focus on our objectives, we will not let ourselves be disheartened by the envy of others. Still, those negative feelings can at times sway us, no doubt about that.

Any time we want to turn on a light, there are those who will try to suppress it, even when they are also hampered by darkness. They are stuck in the mediocrity trap. Still, to each his own. We can only lament that some people are so misguided.

But the biggest surprise was yet to come. Mr. Adams looked at me intently, and told me, "Francisco, I don't want to just praise you, and massage your ego, because I'm a practical man. As I said, I recognize your effort, and would like to invest in your training. Our firm will pay for your law degree. What do you say?"

I was astonished. I simply did not know what to say, and I had to struggle mightily to contain my tears.

He saw that I was overwhelmed by my emotions. To spare me any embarrassment, he said some more words and dismissed me, saying, "Well, if you're OK with it, let's get back to work, because tomorrow is another day."

When I left the office, I was beside myself with joy. I smiled and cried at the same time.

Some people looked at me oddly, perhaps thinking I was mad. I was overwhelmed with so much generosity, which I was not used to. However, that was my moment, my victory, or at least, the beginning of it!

CHAPTER 14

My Home

There are some things that are really special in our lives. In my case, it was the opportunity to attend a university in the United States. It was a dream I had never imagined that I would realize, and indeed I could not have done it, without the help of the man who would become one of my best friends, perhaps my best friend ever, and to whom I would be eternally grateful.

I was greatly motivated to study law, despite the difficulties in performing my duties at the firm at the same time. Nevertheless, I managed my schedule, and worked very hard to fulfill all my work obligations.

Saturdays, Sundays and holidays were days of work and study. Leisure was a luxury I could not afford anymore, since I was involved up to my neck in professional and academic activities.

My only entertainment was studying. Yet, in spite of the

tiredness, the improper diet, and the few hours of sleep, things were going well, and I was thrilled.

My financial situation improved, due to a raise I received, but also because of my lifestyle. After all, if there was one advantage of not having any leisure time, it was that I did nothing that was costing me money.

I thought it was time to make some changes in my life, and started looking for an apartment to rent. I wanted to have my own things. I was not picky, or a consumerist, but I needed to have my space, and preserve my individuality.

I always believed in the teachings of Jesus, and in the old verse, "Help yourself and Heaven will help you." It was an undeniable truth, because the universe always contrives in favor of those who have a strong desire to improve themselves, and improve their community.

After a few weeks of searching, I found a suitable place. Despite being very small, for me it was a real mansion when compared to my tiny room in the Cuban's house.

The apartment was cozy, and had simple furniture. It only needed to be painted and given a good cleaning. Mario and his wife helped me and, before long, my new home was ready to receive me.

Mario also helped me move my few belongings, which basically consisted of books, three suits, and a few other things.

At some point, he told me, "Francisco, I really like what I'm seeing, and I'm very happy for you. For someone who came here cutting grass, you improved your life a lot, and very quickly, no? Keep working hard, don't ever give up. When we believe in our dreams and fight for them, our success comes more easily."

"Thank you, my friend! I'm pretty happy too. I feel I'm making progress and learning, and I owe you a lot for that."

"You owe me nothing, Francisco. When I got here, I met people who also helped me become who I am today. I try to do the same when I get the chance. I have plenty to be grateful for in my life, and I seek, in many ways, to give back."

Meditating on his words, I thought of my work. I dealt with people who, like me, sought to put down roots in American soil. I remembered meeting several clients who went through severe hardships. I realized that, without a doubt, I performed my work efficiently. However, I definitely could have been more sensitive, more humane, more caring and motivating. I could have done more for those people, in the same way that Mario and Mr. Adams had done for me. An alarm sounded in my head, and at that moment, I decided to change my behavior. I had received a lot, and it was time to give back.

Still feeling the impact of those thoughts, I looked at my friend and promised, "I'll follow your example, Mario.

Whenever I can, I'll try to be more useful, and help people. Thank you for everything."

Emotionally, we hugged each other. Silently, we loaded his pickup truck with my few belongings.

My new home beckoned, crowning my list of achievements.

I was wrapped in mixed feelings of joy and melancholy. I reviewed my life, as if it were a movie, and I saw how much it had changed. I had travelled a path I did not even know existed. I had faced many fights and battles. Some I lost, and some I won. But on balance, I won much more than I lost, and that made me feel a wonderful taste of victory and achievement.

While in a retrospective mood, thinking of what happened in my life the last three years, I noted the following.

I moved to an unknown country, with nothing but might and courage. I was penniless, and did not speak the language. I had a college degree, but could not practice my profession. I was without family, counting only one single friend. In so little time, I had arranged a promising job in my professional field. I got real friends and a home. On top of all that, I was attending an American university, which would offer me opportunities for growth and a secure career. My God! What else could I possibly want?

CHAPTER 15

Matters of the Heart

My life became more comfortable after I moved to my new home. The apartment was strategically located near the office and the university, greatly facilitating the management of my commitments and my schedule.

I made only a few friends in college. I was older than most students, and had little in common with them, their parties, conversations and behavior. Of course, I completely understood and respected them, since I was young once, although my youth was lived in very different circumstances.

My group of colleagues and friends included an American girl named Jennifer. She was friendly, cheerful, and very committed to her studies. Her generosity, kindness, and willingness to help other people stood out. She was a member of the student government, and was engaged in various social projects, promoted by the university.

One day, she came to me, looking for legal advice. She knew I worked in a law firm specializing in immigration law. In one of her visits, promoted by a social project sponsored by the university, she met a family which needed legal assistance. Remembering my conversation with Mario, I recognized that life always provides us with the opportunity to serve, and decided to help them.

After that, we became friends. We got together whenever we could. I always felt an immense connection with her. We did not compete; we collaborated with each other. We talked for hours, about all sorts of subjects, and we always felt that we could talk for even longer. We studied together, which helped me a lot, since my time was severely limited.

Jennifer was a typical American girl, younger than me, but very mature for her age. Slowly, I felt a different type of feeling growing in my heart. But I tried to suppress it, since I had other priorities. I promised myself I would do everything I could to excel in my work and in my studies. I owed it to Mr. Adams. I was determined to repay his generosity with my gratitude, and my full commitment. I would not allow anything to distract me, or to change my focus.

Deep down, there were other reasons. I felt rather

insecure about my feelings and my love life.

Until then, I had only had a few romantic relationships in Brazil, but nothing serious. Perhaps, as a matter of defense, I had developed a coldness that prevented me from becoming seriously committed to anyone. For one reason or another, I was abandoned by everyone I loved, and the defense mechanism I found was to build a wall, thus avoiding the grief of losing someone ever again.

One day, Jennifer told me she had won tickets to a basketball game, and invited me to watch it with her in a stadium in downtown Miami. I accepted, thinking that other colleagues would go too.

I was a little surprised to see that there was no one else. We had never met outside the college. We only talked on campus, or by phone and e-mail. I had always avoided anything like a date, because I sensed that she was interested in me, at least a little bit. Our friendship was so precious, and made me so happy, that I did not want to risk losing it over a romantic relationship that might not work.

On our way to the stadium, I asked her, "You did not invite our colleagues to come to the game?"

"Yes, I did. But they're all going to one of those parties that we don't like much, so it'll be just the two of us. Do you mind?"

"No, of course not," I lied shamelessly.

I did not know what was happening to me. We often talked alone, but that day I felt that there was something different. I asked myself, what is the problem with watching a game at her side, in the middle of a crowd? Yet, my heart was racing, and my hands were cold and trembling.

We entered the stadium, and found our places. After we sat down, carrying our soda and popcorn, filled with all the calories we were entitled to, I slowly started to relax, and enjoyed the game. It was the first time I had watched a basketball game live, and it was the national championship final, which made it even more exciting. I could feel the exhilaration of the fans every time points were scored.

I had some fun, for the first time in a while, and I fell in love with this sport, which would captivate me for the rest of my life.

When we left, she said she needed to go back home, because her uncles from New York were visiting, having arrived that day. She asked if I needed a ride, but I thought it was best to refuse, to avoid causing her any delay.

When we said our goodbyes, her lips, whether by accident or deliberately, brushed mine. I immediately felt as if an electric shock hit me. We parted quickly and awkwardly.

I went home that night with my head in the clouds. I could not stop thinking about her.

We continued our friendship and our chats, never mentioning that incident. A few days later, she invited me for a barbecue, at her house. I thought it was a great opportunity to get to know her family. I always looked forward to meeting Americans, and the chance to improve my knowledge of their culture and customs. Being introduced to new people was something I really enjoyed.

Following the advice of a coworker, I brought a beautiful flower bouquet for Jennifer's mother, our hostess, and thus observed the rules of etiquette for the occasion.

When I got near Jennifer's address, I noticed that the neighborhood was much more upscale than the ones I had visited before. Elegant mansions were positioned at the edge of numerous canals and lakes. Boats and yachts were moored behind the houses, as if they were cars in a garage.

Jennifer and her mother greeted me at the door. The older woman gave me a curious and suspicious look. Her manners were pleasant, but cool.

I got the impression that she was worried, fearful that I would invade her domain. Her demeanor was defensive, as if she were protecting Jennifer, her only child. I took a deep breath and handed her the flowers, trying to be as courteous as possible.

We walked into the pool area, which resembled a club to me, not only because of its large size, but also because of its furniture and décor.

Her father was at the grill. Barbecue was his specialty, and he loved cooking it whenever he could. He was extremely polite and gentlemanly, trying to put me at ease and to make me comfortable.

We sat under an umbrella, and the mother started our conversation. She inquired about my life, seeking to get as much information about me as possible. She was putting me through an interrogation, which was done tactfully, but she had so many questions that it made me uncomfortable.

Jennifer tried to hide her embarrassment, perhaps because she had not expected that type of reaction. My intuition told me that it was my Latin American appearance that was causing the hostility. But I was an attorney, after all, and thus I employed my skills with words to tactfully quench her mother's curiosity.

Calmly, I told them about my background, how I had arrived in the United States, where I lived, what I was doing with my life, and so on.

She was very astute, always keeping her cool manners while interrogating me.

Jennifer's father finally got me out of the ordeal, calling me over to stand beside him at the grill. Being very friendly, he asked, "What do you think of the interrogation? My wife sometimes likes to give people the third degree." He smiled. "You know how those supermoms are, no?"

Trying to relax, I answered, "Your wife was very kind, and we had a very pleasant conversation." But at the same time, I thought to myself: Yeah, right! A Nazi general might not even have pumped me so fiercely.

The lunch was without incident. Jennifer's father, always showing a good sense of humor, sought to create a friendlier atmosphere, and to put me at ease. The mother looked calm. I do not know whether she was being sincere, or if she was just pretending, not wanting to be more intrusive than she had already been.

After lunch, they both went to the kitchen, to fetch dessert. I found it odd, since there were several servants in the house, always available, and I was the only visitor. After a few minutes, Jennifer's father, Peter, went to the bathroom, while I headed to the kitchen to offer my help, not out of curiosity, but because I wanted to be solicitous.

I walked through a huge room, and when I started to enter the kitchen, I realized that I was the subject of the conversation between Jennifer and her mother, Caroline. They did not notice my presence, and unfortunately, I could hear their words.

"How can you bring this guy to our house, Jennifer? He's just a poor immigrant, without anybody to vouch for him!"

"Mom," Jennifer replied, "Don't be a bigot. He's my

friend, and a very special person."

I cleared my throat, to announce my presence. Pretending that nothing happened, I asked if everything was all right, and if I could be of any assistance. They were both surprised. Caroline looked deeply annoyed and embarrassed. She busied herself with the cutlery, issuing orders to one of the servants.

I did my best to remain unperturbed. I was, once again, facing the cold and brutal reality of dealing with prejudice. "Immigrants are this, immigrants are that," people proclaim, as if we all could be defined by one single adjective.

I thought about saying something, but good manners and common sense prevailed. After all, Caroline was in her house, and it would not be a good idea to confront her in her territory. She might become defensive and insulting.

Prudently, I decided to bide my time, and return her just deserts when the opportunity presented itself.

Jennifer, mortified, apologized, stating that her mother was a difficult person, but had a good heart. Seeing her dejection, I felt sorry for her. I did not want her to suffer on my account.

We savored our dessert in a tranquil atmosphere. My host, who was much more considerate to me, served us coffee accompanied by delicious chocolate.

A few hours later, I needed to leave. Monday waited

for me, and I still had to organize some things, and review some notes, just trivial stuff.

I said goodbye to Peter, exchanging the usual pleasantries. He was still very friendly to me. Then, I said goodbye to Jennifer. But, when I said goodbye to Caroline, I saw an opening to throw her rudeness right back at her.

She walked me to the door, declaring, "It was very nice meeting you, and we look forward to having you back."

I felt the utter lack of sincerity in her words. I did not want to sound arrogant or uncivil, but I would not tolerate being treated as a "nobody" yet again.

Using a low, but firm tone, and with a broad smile on my face, I answered, "I doubt you're really looking forward to seeing me again, since, as you said yourself, I'm just an immigrant!"

She did not say a word, since she knew very well what I meant. I was rather pleased with myself, knowing she would remember me for a very long time.

CHAPTER 16

Values

Unwittingly, Caroline did me a big favor. Her bias against me triggered a healthy dose of self-esteem. It led me to a revelation, not about how others saw me, but how I saw myself, which greatly improved my life from then on.

Our perception of life is subjective. It is colored by our feelings, experiences and values. We are what we believe we are. I discovered at that moment that, despite declaring that I was equal to others, deep down I did not see myself that way. The prejudice was inside me.

I remember my father explaining that I should not consider myself inferior to anyone because I was poor, because what really counted was my character, that was what distinguished people. At that time I did not quite understand what my father was trying to teach me. Today, I know that he talked about moral values, about being good, fair and honest.

We are all immigrants. We are just passing on Earth, literally. We immigrated to this planet, but we will not stay for long. The life span of homo sapiens, whether 90 or 100 years, is negligible when compared to the evolutionary process that has been going on for millions of years.

It is common to say, when someone lived for 100 years, "He lived a very long life."

A very long life? According to whom?

Having arrived at these conclusions, I began to plan my next move, regarding my career. After all, the United States was the land of opportunity for professionals who excelled in their respective fields, even if they were not natives. Well, it was time to move up to another stage in my career. It was not a matter of vanity, but of justice, and of enhancing my potential. If I continued to behave like a worthless immigrant, a loser, that was how I would be treated by others. Needless to say, I did not have the slightest interest in positioning myself as a loser.

I decided to schedule a meeting with Mr. Adams to discuss some things that were going on with my job. I wanted to talk about the various unimportant or insignificant cases that are routinely directed to me because no one else wanted them; about the bureaucratic matters that always ended up in my hands; and of course, I wanted to talk about the fact that I still had to pick up lunch for other people. I did not intend to go into details, to avoid compromising my colleagues, but I wanted to let him know about those situations. I was determined to change my whole attitude towards my work.

It was not that I did not want to be helpful, since kindness generated kindness, but many coworkers abused my good will, and my subordinate position, to burden me with tasks that did not belong to me.

Essentially, I became more aware of my potential, my professional skills, and the strength of my character.

While I waited for the meeting, I followed my daily routine. Jennifer continued to treat me in the same way as before, which greatly pleased me. I was even more enchanted by her mature behavior.

We talked about the incident at her house. Tactfully, she declared, "I want to apologize for my mother's inappropriate behavior. I completely understand if you're upset."

"Absolutely not," I replied. "In fact, your mother has no idea of the favor she has done for me. She helped me get myself out of my exile, and made me see the important things in my life."

I continued, "Suddenly, I got ashamed of the way I was living, so to speak, and started to pay more attention to myself. I was living the life of an unskilled servant. Surely, the distorted way I saw myself was caused by my background and social status, which were very poor. However, I'm capable and worthy. I realized that those capitalist-oriented beliefs, that no one is irreplaceable, are in fact a form of manipulation, designed to frighten, especially those with poor self-esteem."

I concluded, "Regardless of what we do, we are all, in a sense, irreplaceable. Others can perhaps do it better, but they will do it differently, because we are alike, but not identical."

"I agree with you, Francisco. But those feelings were sparked by disrespectful behavior? How can that be?"

"Actually, those feelings were always deep inside me. I have been fooling myself for a long time. Often, we value ourselves based on what we have, and not what we are. Many people place a lot of importance on one's address, car, bank account, trips, and other material things. However, these things do not define what we are, you know that."

"We value the external form, but not the essence, isn't that so?" she interjected.

"That's right! I'm not disregarding material things, and I'll not give up the chance to live well. But I don't need to be a slave to my possessions. I'll master them instead. Bob Marley was right, when he said that "God gives us people to love and things to use, not things to love and people to use."

Finally, the day of my meeting with Mr. Adams arrived. He was attentive and engaged, as always.

"Hello, Francisco. How is our soon-to-be attorney?"

"I'm fine, sir. How are you?"

"I'm well. What can I do for you?"

I wanted to be brief, so I said to him, "Nothing much, sir. I'll get right to the point, because I don't want to take too much of your time, I know how busy you are. It's about the work I've been doing here at the office."

"Is there a problem, Francisco?"

"Well, I wouldn't call it a problem, sir, not really. However, I'd like to make a few adjustments. When I started my job here at the office, I knew, and fully accepted, that I had to learn and be trained. Thus, I was responsible for the bureaucratic paperwork, and I was routinely assigned the simplest, least interesting cases."

"There's nothing unusual in that," I continued. "But my colleagues are still passing on to me the cases they have no interest in doing. In addition, I still have to do the work of an office-boy, making deliveries and picking up lunch for them. It's not that I find it demeaning. I want to make clear that I'm not complaining about my work, but about things that I consider unfair and abusive."

"Sir, I want to change those things. I'll be pleasant and

helpful, of course, but I want to do things differently from now on. Knowing human nature, I'm aware that those changes could upset some colleagues. So, I wanted to warn you in advance, because I worry that their dissatisfaction may negatively influence your opinion of me."

He completely surprised me with his answer.

"Francisco, I understand completely. I was just waiting for you to come and talk to me. I have observed many times the things you mentioned. But you had to take the initiative and build your self-confidence. I didn't interfere because I didn't want to make matters worse for you. Don't worry about office gossip, that's unavoidable. Just keep doing your work, because, as the old Arab saying teaches us, "The dogs bark, but the caravan moves on.""

CHAPTER 17

Guava Paste, Once Again

Time flew. Two years passed in the blink of an eye. My graduation was near. Jennifer and I grew even closer to each other.

We spent a lot of time together. She was indeed a great friend, and a loyal companion. Actually, it was much more than that. We were totally enthralled with each other. At the end of our last term, we were officially dating. Our colleagues, who believed we were just good friends, were astonished, but happy for us.

Gradually, she knocked down all the walls that I had erected around me. She showed me that true love is simple and good. We are the ones that complicate things. I worked through things, overcoming my fear of a serious relationship, and my fear of losing her and being left alone once again.

Mario gifted me with a Spiritist[4] book of messages, psychographed[5] by a Brazilian medium called Francisco Cândido Xavier. In one of its messages, dictated by the Spiritual Author Emmanuel[6], I found a sentence that stirred something in my heart. It stated that "The only love we have is the one we give away." It sounded to me like the absolute truth. We can only feel the love that is in our heart.

Love does not end with death or distance. When true, it survives everything. We are the ones that cannot survive without love.

We commit to love, and we build love. In my life, love was a work in progress. In some cases, the work was just starting, and there was much to do yet. For instance,

---

4 The term Spiritist is related to the word Spiritism, which is a philosophical, scientific and religious doctrine codified in the 19th century by the French educator Hippolyte Léon Denizard Rivail (Lyon, October 3, 1804 – Paris, March 31, 1869), using the pen name Allan Kardec. The five books, published by Kardec, which constitute the Spiritist Codification, are: The Spirits' Book (Le Livre des Esprits); The Mediums' Book (Le Livre des Médiums); The Gospel According to Spiritism (L'Évangile Selon le Spiritisme); Heaven and Hell (Le Ciel et L'Enfer); The Genesis According to Spiritism (La Genèse).

5 According to the concept created by Allan Kardec, psychography is the writing of spirits by a medium's hand. See The Mediums' Book, by Allan Kardec, Paris, 1861.

6 The Spiritual author, Emmanuel, was the spirit that dictated the message, which was written through the hand of the medium Francisco Cândido Xavier.

I still needed to establish an amicable relationship with Jennifer's mother, my future mother-in-law.

While our friends were happy to see Jennifer and me together, Caroline most definitely was not. I wondered what went through her mind when she learned about our relationship, that her wonderful, American daughter was dating a penniless immigrant like me. What a waste, she probably thought.

I just shrugged. I was not worried about what people thought about me anymore. Fortunately, my girlfriend had the same attitude. She was very mature, and did not bow to any family pressure. That strength of character was exactly what I expected from her. I needed someone strong beside me, and I was glad I had found her. I firmly believe in the old saying, "Behind every great man there is a great woman," and vice-versa.

Some people from the firm attended my graduation, including Mr. Adams and his family. My Cuban friend Mario, and his team, as he referred to his wife and seven children, also came.

Jennifer graduated as well. Most of her family and friends were there. To her mother's despair, she happily introduced me to every single one of them, without exception, as her boyfriend.

It was a very emotional moment. Mr. Adams was

elated, and told me that after that achievement, the bar exam, which was the equivalent of the Brazilian bar exam, waited for me. With my strong will and determination, he remarked, I would overcome that challenge easily.

I always appreciated words of encouragement from this man, who was like a father figure to me, since I had lost my dad. Each day, I admired him more.

Growing up without a father is especially hard when we are little children. We sorely need our dad's guidance and example. However, when we are adults without a father, what we really miss is a dependable shoulder we can lean on, someone we can talk to, and exchange experiences with. Most of all, we miss the joy of sharing our successes and failures with those who gave us the greatest gift of all, our very existence.

But it was a time for celebration, and a big surprise awaited me. Mr. Adams invited everyone to his house, because he had planned a party for me. I really was not expecting that. Most of the office staff awaited us there.

I was not able to contain my joy and emotion. At that moment, I returned to my childhood, and remembered Mr. Roberto and my father. Ah, if they could see me! They would know that I was conquering something truly wonderful, like a piece of guava paste, the delicious treat that symbolized the good things in life when I was a little boy growing up with them.

Jennifer went to her parents' house with her relatives and friends. I thought her mother would have a heart attack, when she saw us kiss our goodbyes as a happy and very much in love couple. We were ecstatic, not only for having graduated, but above all, because our love had survived all our differences.

She also had to take the bar exam, so we agreed that, as soon as we graduated, we would not waste any time, and would start preparing for it immediately.

After four months focusing exclusively on our studies, we became like zombies. We decided to take our exam in New York, because, if we passed, we would be able to practice law in a larger area within the United States. If we took the exam in Florida, we would be a little more restricted.

The exam took two full days, and it was much harder than I had anticipated. However, we left confident that we had both done well. We needed to wait for almost twenty days to receive our result and our scores.

While we waited, Jennifer encouraged me all the time, saying proudly, "Look, you took the exam, and I'm sure you did well. This exam isn't for just anyone. Besides, you had to do it in a second language, no less! I really admire you, my love. You are a great example for many people, including me. Not long ago, you were a simple assistant gardener. That's what I call determination!"

The twenty days passed very slowly, like an eternity. I would awake at night, thinking about the exam, about my score, and could not sleep any more. But finally, we accessed the online system with our I.D. numbers and saw the result. We had passed!

I became very emotional. Through tears, I told Jennifer, "I can't believe this is happening. I came here hoping to succeed, but I had no idea what waited for me. But God gave me so much more. He gave me the ability to rise above myself, and he gave me you, the love of my life!"

I called Mr. Adams, and told him the news. He also got very emotional, and told me, "Congratulations! I had no doubt you could do it. Forgive my sentimentality. I think I'm starting to get old."

We both cried on the phone.

The next day, when I got to the office, I was applauded and congratulated by Mr. Adams and by my colleagues.

But other challenges waited for me. It was time to apply for a permanent resident status, commonly known as the 'green card', something I was already late in doing. It was a fundamental step for my career in the United States.

After completing all the appropriate procedures and submitting the required documents, I received my protocol. I followed the process through the U.S. Citizenship and

Immigration Services (USCIS) website, with great anxiety.

It took about twenty days to get the result. Once again, I almost died of excitement when I saw that my request had been approved. I gave a shout of joy in my office, and several colleagues came in thinking I was sick or something.

Everyone cheered when I gave them the news.

I was enormously thrilled to have my application approved. I had only felt a similar joy when I graduated. Obtaining the green card represented a major step for me, because I had already decided to stay in the United States permanently.

I called Jennifer, who already had a job. She worked with her uncle at his law firm. We celebrated over the phone.

Then, I called Mario, who immediately declared that we needed to celebrate with a *puerco asado guajiro*[7], a typical Cuban dish, which he prepared very well.

Soon afterwards, Mr. Adams arrived in the office, after a meeting with one of our clients. Seeing the buzz, he approached us, wanting to know what happened. When he heard the news, he congratulated me, and told me, "Francisco, you really make me proud. Your strength and determination have always impressed me."

When I thanked him, he countered, "You know, I'm the one who should thank you, because your achievements

_____
7 Seasoned roasted pork.

are an inspiration to everyone around here. You brought so much joy to our office, not only because of your hard work and dedication, but especially by your easygoing, cheerful disposition. Don't ever change, my son. May God bless you and enlighten your path."

He talked to me like a real father, even blessing me. I answered with a heartfelt "Amen!"

CHAPTER 18

A Bizarre Client Interview

I t was late afternoon on a Thursday, and I still had to take one last client interview. I had had a particularly stressful day. The deadlines of several cases overlapped, making the paperwork even more burdensome. Everything had to be submitted to the Immigration Services on the following day. However, the motto of our law firm was to never leave the client waiting, and never, except in cases of extreme urgency, cancel a meeting.

I went to the reception room, greeted the client, a Brazilian man called Gregorio, and led him to one of our meeting rooms. He was accompanied by a woman much younger than he, which he introduced to me as his wife, Jacqueline. She was a gorgeous woman, but displayed rather extravagant taste. Her clothes, shoes, jewelry and handbag were quite flashy. They were all from very expensive brands.

Not that I cared. On the contrary, I was always careful to avoid any biased thinking. But really, the woman's ensemble was outlandish. Still, the purpose of our meeting was to consult about legal matters, not fashion. As they say in the United States, time is money, and I had no intention of wasting any of it.

We settled down. I noticed that they were in a hurry, perhaps with some other matters to attend to after our meeting, so I started our consultation right away.

"How can I help you? Our assistant mentioned that you'd like to open a business here in the United States. Is that so?"

"That's right, Mr. Martins. It's a modeling agency. Our target is the fashion industry. We have many investments in this area. Basically, we discover new talents, and through our contacts with other agencies worldwide, we send our models abroad. As you may be aware, Brazilian girls are enormously successful in this line of work, not just for their beauty, but especially because of their talent and resourcefulness."

"I don't really follow the fashion world," I replied, "But I've heard about those models. Our racial miscegenation produced a very beautiful people, if I may say so."

"Indeed, Mr. Martins." He seemed pleased with the fact that I had understood what he was looking for, and continued, "As I was saying, we want to open an agency here. It'd be a subsidiary of the one we have in Brazil, which has been operating for five years or so."

"Do you have any business partner in this venture? If so, would any of them be interested in immigrating to this country as well?"

"I have two more partners, but they'll continue to manage the business in Brazil, while I dedicate myself to the agency here."

"Have you set up the company already? Is it operating?"

"Yes. We found a good location, and started our operations about two months ago. The investment will be approximately two million dollars, overall. We'll spend it on things such as setting up our business facilities and hiring our staff. We need professionals in the areas of photography, filming, marketing, and so on."

"Right. You intend to apply for a work permit, is that correct?"

"Exactly. I'd like to know if we're allowed to get a work permit under those circumstances."

"I don't see any problem in getting a work permit, especially considering the size of the business you're opening. An investment of this magnitude means that the agency in Brazil is doing very well."

"Indeed, we're doing great!"

144 | Umberto Fabbri

"Have you and your wife have ever lived abroad?"

"Oh yes. We travel a lot. For many years, we have been keeping a house here in Miami. That's because we love the Florida lifestyle. So, adaptation won't be a problem. We live, or rather, we spend a lot of time here, taking care of business, but also enjoying some leisure time, such as deep-sea fishing. I really love boating."

"Very well, sir. I have here a short list of documents, required by the American Immigration Services, which I'd like to review with you."

He made a bored expression. His wife also seemed anxious to get out of there. She had been staring out the window the whole time, as if seeking for something more interesting than the conversation we were having.

He replied quickly, "My assistant will help you deal with the paperwork. She'll come to see you, OK?"

He got up, shook my hand, and left immediately.

I do not know what came over me, but when I greeted him, I felt that there was something strange about him. Simply put, he did not emit a good vibration. Perhaps I was just too tired in that late afternoon. Still, I thought it was strange that a businessman would come and deal with those matters personally, considering that he had an assistant to handle those details. An individual who would invest two million dollars in a business venture in the

United States would take care of those issues in person?

In my job, I dealt with people from all walks of life. But usually, the big fish, as we used to say, did not handle those initial interviews personally, we only met them at the end of the proceedings to finalize matters. Besides, we were the ones that usually went to see them, in their offices, homes or hotels. It was rare to conduct an initial interview with someone so wealthy.

Maybe I was just imagining things, but I did not have a good feeling about the situation. The next morning, I received a call from a man who introduced himself as Mr. Gregório's assistant, requesting the list of documents.

I was intrigued, once again. I was under the impression that the assistant was a woman. Well, maybe I was mistaken. After all, it had been a long and tiring day. Perhaps Mr. Gregorio had told me it was a male assistant, and I had heard the exact opposite.

A few days later, the assistant called me again. He wanted to deliver some of the documents. We scheduled a meeting, almost at the end of my workday.

He arrived an hour late, but did not express any regret for his lack of punctuality. He had a somewhat sinister appearance, and gave me the impression that he was hiding something. He greeted me quickly, and told me that his name was Rafael.

Then, he handed me the documents, and a small, nicely wrapped box, saying, "Mr. Gregorio asked me to deliver it to you. It's a gift, in recognition of your commitment to the process."

A gift? But for what? I did not do anything beyond conducting a quick consultation. Furthermore, the company's policy was very clear on the issue of gifts. Our business ethics recommended that we not accept them. If the situation became too awkward for the client, we would receive the gift, but we would send it to the Human Resources Department, who would donate it to a charity.

"There is no need to give me any gifts. It's my pleasure, as well as my responsibility, to assist you."

"Nonsense!" He exclaimed. "Open it and see if you like it. Mr. Gregorio insists."

I thought that his behavior was rude. He presented himself as an assistant, but treated me as if I were a mere intern.

I realized that the situation could become even more awkward, and opened the box. I was very surprised by what I found. It was a very expensive pen. The glint of metal suggested it was gold plated.

I started to refuse it, but he just glared at me. He stood up, bade me an informal farewell, and left in a haste.

I handed the gift to the HR Department. As I was

returning to my office, I met Mr. Adams, who invited me to a quick coffee.

During our coffee, I briefly told him what had happened. Very calmly, he gave some advice.

"Pay close attention to the documentation, and to any conversation you have with this client. We can never, as attorneys, go against our intuition. It's part of our training, isn't it? If your intuition is saying that something is wrong, stay tuned."

The next morning, the situation took another odd turn. I had not even opened the envelope that had been delivered by Mr. Gregório's assistant, containing the documents, when I received a call from a special agent from the Florida police, who wanted to see me. He told me it was an urgent matter. We scheduled our meeting for the same day, shortly after lunchtime.

I decided it would be prudent to include a fellow attorney in our meeting. It would be good to have a more experienced colleague with me, who could also serve as a witness to the proceedings, since I had never faced a situation like that, and did not know what to expect.

Right on time, our receptionist announced that a Mr. Richard B. had arrived. I thought it was best to welcome him personally. He was accompanied by two gentlemen.

We went to the meeting room, and they formally

introduced themselves, showing their badges and identity documents. They were two special agents and an immigration officer.

My colleague, Bob, joined us. I made the introductions quickly, without asking if they had any objection to his attending the meeting. Since they did not say anything, I started our conversation.

"Well, gentlemen, what can I do for you?"

"Our purpose here is to obtain some information about a client of yours," answered Special Agent Richard B., who seemed to be the officer in charge of the operation.

"We detained an individual called Gregorio, his wife, his assistant, Rafael, and a number of people who said they're working for him. They have been investigated for the crime of human trafficking. We would like to know what kind of business they were conducting with your law firm."

I knew there was something wrong with that couple and with the so-called assistant, I thought. My intuition was right!

I answered, "Those individuals came to see us, seeking information on the requirements and procedures for a work permit application."

I described my meeting with Mr. Gregorio and his wife, as well as my meeting with the assistant, Rafael. I told them about the envelope with the documents, and the gift they gave me.

The special agent showed us a warrant, requesting the documents that Mr. Gregorio had already admitted to the Police that he had delivered to us.

I handed over the envelope while Bob retrieved the pen from the HR Department. Meanwhile, I repeated to myself an old Brazilian saying, "The more I pray, the more the ghosts haunt me."

Another case was assigned to me that turned out to be a minefield. Definitely, I was becoming an expert in handling the hot potatoes, while my colleagues usually got the crème de la crème.

It was a messy, unsavory affair. Clearly, I needed to distance our law firm from Gregorio and his cohorts.

When Bob returned to the room, I resumed the conversation.

"Well, the situation looks extremely serious. However, we were completely unaware of their real activities. Anyway, we are, of course, at your disposal, should you require any further clarifications. But we would like to avoid, and now I speak on behalf of our law firm, any publicity in relation to this case. Obviously, we have no interest in any kind of negative information associating us with the issue of human trafficking. Also, there are confidentiality issues to consider. We don't want to tarnish our good name."

Agent Richard B. replied. "Don't worry, Mr. Martins.

The suspects provided us all the information we need regarding their dealings with your law firm. Besides, you have a strong reputation of integrity. There won't be any problem."

Indeed, there was no mention of us when the situation came to light. The media reported that the operation was large. The gang had made millions with human and drug trafficking, and other minor crimes.

They had a fake agency operating in Brazil and in the United States. They lured young boys and girls with the promise that they could have a successful career, working on the runways, or as photographic or commercial models. However, when they arrived in the United States, they confiscated their passports under the pretext of getting their work permits. Then, they were forced to do slave work and to consume drugs. After they had become heavily addicted, they were led into prostitution. Many were moved to other countries. It was horrifying. Those victims were subject to a real nightmare. I was deeply outraged. It was hard to accept that things like that could happen, and that some people could be so cold and brutal, treating human beings as if they were commodities.

A few days later, I read the details of the case in the papers. I was rather pleased with the outcome. Those people belonged in prison. They also had lost all their wealth, which had been earned with the exploitation and slavery of others. Now, they were caged like ferocious animals.

My aggressive instincts came to the fore, and I surprised myself with my wrathful thoughts. Awash with indignation, I wondered aloud, "People like that don't deserve to go to jail; they should be shot by a firing squad."

At that exact moment, Mr. Adams entered my office, and upon hearing me, he remarked, "Don't let your emotions take control of you. Who do you want to send to a firing squad?"

It was amazing how in tune we were. I felt like he could read my thoughts and decipher my emotions. Really, I wondered, if reincarnation does in fact exist, then this man must have been my father in another lifetime.

CHAPTER 19

Proposal

My job was going quite well. I got another pay raise, and started to receive a small bonus over the client revenue I generated at the firm.

Then, on a beautiful late afternoon, Mr. Adams came to my office, asking if he could sit down for a bit.

Of course, it was always a great pleasure talking with him, not because he was the leader of our law firm, but because I held him in high regard. I could sense that he reciprocated that feeling.

He asked me, "How are things going, Francisco? Is everything all right with you, with Jennifer, with your life?"

"Sir, things couldn't be better. After graduating from law school, passing the bar exam, and obtaining my green card, I got a new lease on life. Perhaps it's just an emotional boost, because my self-esteem is improving, but whatever it is, it's certainly working."

He smiled happily, and as always, went straight to the point.

"You know, Francisco, I have always had a feeling for people, and thank God, I usually have a good eye for talent. I can recognize it right away. I've been thinking about you, and I'd like to make a proposal, all right?"

I was surprised, but managed to keep my anxiety under control. What type of proposal was he talking about?

I just nodded, and he continued.

"I've made the same proposal to other attorneys, who, like you, have excelled. Basically, the idea is to set up an independent law practice, in which you'll be the major partner, and our law firm will have a small share. Our firm provides the start-up capital, and you perform the actual work. You'll work exclusively in the new office. It'll be a great investment for us, because I'm sure that we'll have a profitable return soon. In addition, we'll be able to diversify our services. On top of all that, I get an intense personal gratification when I contribute directly to the transformation of a brilliant employee to a successful entrepreneur, who, in turn, will maximize his achievements, creating jobs and offering new opportunities to so many others."

He added. "One of the basic tenets for Christians is "Do unto others as you would have others do unto you." Isn't that so?"

There I was, once again, making a huge effort not to burst into tears and look like a crying baby in front of that wonderful man. I reflected on how immensely fortunate I was to cross paths with Mr. Adams. What type of person was that, who sought not only his personal success, but who gave hope and opportunities to others?

Some people argue that angels do not exist. I do not know. But at that moment, Mr. Adams looked like a real angel to me. I had no doubt that he had been sent by my father and by my friend Mr. Roberto to be my guardian angel.

I sought to compose myself, and answered him, "Mr. Adams, I have no words to thank you. I promise that you'll never regret this opportunity you're giving me. I'll do everything that is possible, and even the impossible, to make sure that this law practice is your best investment ever!"

Mr. Adams, with his usual good humor, stood up, extended his hand to greet me, and declared, jokingly, "If you don't have words to thank me, then don't thank me."

Before he left the room, I told him goodbye. I confess I made a huge effort to not kiss his hands, which would make me look sappy, or give the impression that I wanted to ingratiate myself with him, something I disliked.

I believed that good manners, politeness and ethics

are essential in all occasions, especially when allied with competency and the willingness to do one's best. As such, I always considered flattery unnecessary. Many argue that the world is a political place, and I agree. But flattery, to me, is politicking at its worst, it's fawning. Still, to each his own. Besides, there is no accounting for taste; we can only regret it.

My mind, however, was in a whirl!

My God, I would have my own law practice, and Jennifer could work with me, if she wanted, since she handled many immigration cases at her uncle's firm.

A golden opportunity was handed to me, and for sure, I would grab it, and do everything in my power to succeed.

CHAPTER 20

A Challenging Start

I was always eager to pursue new paths in my professional career. Since I was offered an opportunity to set up a law practice of my own, with the support of John Adams, I decided that the best course of action was to seek office space. It had to be affordable, but in a good location. Moreover, it must have suitable facilities, so it would not look shabby. I needed a tasteful place to attract distinguished clients.

I found it in a new building, not too far from my old firm. It had enough space for a reception room, a meeting room, and two offices. Best of all, I could rent it for a reasonable price.

I prepared the paperwork, and signed the contract, which was endorsed by Mr. Adams. He really liked the place. As always, he encouraged my choices.

I officially resigned from my former law firm, and moved

to the new office a few weeks later.

Jennifer loved the place, and I immediately invited her to work with me. She accepted, but requested some time to close her cases at her uncle's firm before transferring.

I thought that everything was great. I started to offer my services to the people I knew, my acquaintances, college friends and professors. Like any start-up business, there were times in the day when I did not have anything significant to do. Thus, I decided to visit large companies. I wanted to open doors as quickly as possible.

I met a good marketing professional, who prepared appropriate materials. I also asked Mr. Adams for some referrals. After establishing the initial contact with those companies, I would seek more referrals.

As expected, we struggled mightily for almost a year, with only a handful of cases to handle. Jennifer moved to our office. But she, at least, had financial stability because her parents were ready to support her in case she needed it.

Her mother, not surprisingly, disapproved of her decision to leave her uncle's law firm to work with me. One day, Jennifer told me about a quick conversation she had with Caroline.

"How could you do that, Jennifer? You're a girl from a good family, you had a nice job working with your uncle, my brother, and you just leave it all behind for this risky venture with your boyfriend!"

"I have the right to make my choices, Mom. Besides, I'm not starting a risky venture, I'm creating my own space. Relax, don't worry so much."

But Caroline was not mollified, Jennifer said. She was so mad she made a face like she had just eaten a whole bag of sour lemons.

But while Jennifer enjoyed financial stability, I did not. My modest savings were fast disappearing. Even though I was in a partnership with Mr. Adams, I still had to cover the bulk of the office expenses.

Jennifer offered to help. But I could not accept it. It was not a matter of pride. Indeed, I may have many faults, but being too proud is not one of them. A friend jokingly told me once, "A pauper cannot afford to be proud. It's the height of stupidity!" I agree with him completely. I just did not want to leave her in an awkward situation with her parents.

Still, I needed to make enough profit to at least meet the expenses.

Jennifer did not complain. Instead, she got referrals from her father. I got along well with him. He did not allow himself to be influenced by his wife.

She encouraged me, reminding me that starting a new

business is always very difficult. Even those who inherit a business, she argued, have to make an effort to get up to speed and learn to manage it.

My first client came by referral from the director of a large company, to whom I had offered my services previously. His name was Thiago H. Mr. H. was a middle-aged, well-educated Argentinian, who had a solid professional background. He owned a technology company in Buenos Aires, geared specifically toward the real estate industry, and had opened a subsidiary in the United States.

He was quite unhappy with the American Immigration Services, which had twice denied a work permit to one of his company's managers in Buenos Aires, an expert in the sector, who had been working for him for over five years. Mr. H. wanted to bring this employee to the United States, to help him roll-out his business venture in the country.

He needed a skilled technician to oversee the American operations, to act as a liaison between the subsidiary and the parent company, and to train new personnel who would be hired as the business grew.

Immigration Services denied his request, alleging that his operations in the United States were just beginning, and that the revenue produced was too small to justify bringing a professional from another country. The company should hire someone locally.

"It's really absurd," he complained. "How can I grow my business in the United States, if I cannot bring in the right people? I won't find in this country the specialist my company needs. It's not enough to know the technology. The person must be able to understand how our product, which was developed in Argentina, works. If I hire someone here, I would have to invest a lot of money and time, to train him or her and I simply can't afford it. The employee I want to bring here has worked with me for over five years, and knows everything there is to know about our system. So, I cannot accept this refusal."

He added. "The attorney handling my case told me that there was nothing else that could be done. However, I haven't resigned myself to this, and decided to ask for a second opinion, and that was when someone gave me your name."

He continued. "I wonder whether the official that reviewed my application knows anything about the origins of some of the most successful American companies. A slew of technology entrepreneurs started their enterprises in the garages of their homes. Others created their first projects while they were still in college, and so on."

Frustrated at the way his case was handled by Immigration Services, Mr. H. concluded, "I sent bank statements, plus a ton of paper, because it seems that they love paper and bureaucracy. Or maybe they have a paper-eating monster they need to feed. Their response was that my business is too small, that the amount of money in the bank is too modest, and so on."

I waited for him to take a pause, or to say something.

"Mr. H, I understand your indignation. However, in cases like this, the evaluation conducted is similar to the evaluation that is carried out when someone applies for credit. In fact, we can say that credit is being sought, even if it's a "moral credit." Essentially, a start-up business, especially a small one, has to face several hurdles, and may close its doors before completing three years in existence. So, the main concern is that the business might contract debts with other companies that cannot be met, or that it won't be able to pay its employees."

He countered, "Fair enough. But I have a solid, profitable and reputable company in Argentina. So, if what they fear is delinquency, perhaps they could set up a procedure requesting that I make a security deposit. What I don't understand is how they can expect a company's subsidiary, which is just starting its operations in this country, to have better results than the headquarters."

He added, "I came to you, Mr. Martins, because you were highly recommended. I was told that you're often able to successfully close your cases."

"To build a solid application, Mr. H., we have to supply the proper documents, and demonstrate the robustness of your company, without any kind of subterfuge. You need to show things as they are. Furthermore, I suggest you invest in your subsidiary here in the United States. Look, your parent company is solid, but it is in Buenos Aires. The business here in the United States must produce its own revenue. Besides, it must have suitable facilities to hold its operations. Most importantly, it must have customers requesting its services. Then, the business can stand on its own feet, and prove that it's strong and reliable, not just a front company.

"Let's put ourselves in the place of an immigration officer. Do you have partners?"

"Yes, I have two."

"Very well. Who can guarantee that your partners will agree to any transfer of currency, if the venture here in the United States does not go well? It's always an unknown. What about the employees and creditors, will they get what is owed to them from the parent company abroad?"

I continued, "Do you understand? We can prepare another application, but let's first examine the financial issues carefully. You and your partners are willing to invest in the American subsidiary, are you not?"

"We are. We think the American real estate market

offers us excellent opportunities. Our products and services can be a good fit for the construction business, as well as all the other companies operating in this sector. We decided to set up a subsidiary here because our customers in Argentina have many investments in other countries, especially in the United States."

"Then, let's start by injecting capital in the subsidiary, ensuring that all the expenses are comfortably covered, for a two-year period. It must cover administrative costs, employees, suppliers, etc. Do you agree?"

"Sure. We want to invest in this market."

"Very well. First, we demonstrate the integrity and the reliability of your company, and that there is a demand for your products and services. Then we will seek the work permit for your employee, providing all the required documents. I believe that within four to six months, we'll be able to apply. Is that acceptable to you?"

He nodded. And then I added, "Remember, first we have to present real evidence that your company is here to stay, and that you're not visa hunters. I apologize for speaking that way, but I have seen everything, from arranged weddings with Americans to schemes with companies that are only strong on paper."

"I understand, Mr. Martins."

"Of course, there are immigration officers who seem

to have one single purpose: to deny! It's the "Let's deny and see what happens" mentality. I don't agree with that at all. Often, it looks like they want to exert too much power. This behavior makes it look like they don't take their work seriously, but that they exercise an excessive, or unnecessary, caution. Deep down, it only demonstrates a lack of sheer common sense. Obviously, we can't believe that they're all the same. We must analyze things carefully, don't you think?"

"I agree completely. Of course, I can see that they have a huge responsibility. One bad mistake would not only jeopardize their jobs, but can put the safety of a community, whether a big or a small one, at risk."

"Indeed. But as an attorney, I believe that some go too far. It appears that they do not like the fact that foreigners come here. But, if we get to the bottom of the issue, we'll see that countless foreigners have settled here, and are now helping this great nation grow. Maybe their personal contribution is modest, but their sons and daughters are making a difference, and contributing to the social and technological development of this country, and so on."

I noticed that my explanation had calmed him down, and reassured him. Modesty aside, I was becoming good at it.

Some time later, we applied for the work permit on behalf of the employee that Thiago H. wanted to bring from Buenos Aires.

We sent several supporting documents, in addition to bank accounts, income statements, and proof of capital, demonstrating that the American subsidiary had its expenses fully covered. With Jennifer's help, I made a compelling case, arguing that the returns from the parent company in Argentina, and the solidity of the business plan for the subsidiary in the United States proved that the company was robust and reliable.

Less than twenty days later, we learned that the application was approved. My client and I were delighted.

Bit by bit, we moved forward. A lot of effort was required, but because we were thorough in the preparation of our applications, we found no difficulty in getting our cases approved by the Immigration Services.

We started to build a reputation for competence, and the bills began to be paid more easily. Our profit was the reward of our serious and focused work. We did not accept cases that conflicted with our personal and professional standards. Ethics before profit. I have never regretted living that way.

CHAPTER 21

New Clients

B efore too long, we were attracting more clients. Serious work and good results are the best marketing strategies. Word of mouth worked in our favor, and the referrals started to arrive pretty quickly. Soon, Jennifer and I had our hands full. We even talked about the possibility of expanding our firm, and hiring an employee.

Meanwhile, I got a very peculiar case. It was not the circumstances of the case that made it strange, but rather the argument used by the officer from Immigration Services to deny the request.

The client, who was referred by Thiago H., also had a technology company that developed software for the financial industry. Unpretentiously, He introduced himself as Rodrigo and described his case. Like his friend Thiago H., he was opening a subsidiary of his company in the United States, and was very unhappy with the way his case had been handled so far. His work permit application had already received two denials from Immigration Services.

The justifications for the first denial were that his company was just starting its operation, and that he presented an inadequate business plan.

He admitted that he was badly advised, and as result, his business plan left a lot to be desired. Therefore, the denial of his application by the immigration official made perfect sense. He did not want to elaborate further because he was not in the habit of denigrating one professional to another. What he really needed was a work permit, which would allow his company to continue to serve its Brazilian and American clients.

The problem, explained my client, was the reasoning behind the denial of his second application, which he considered to be quite preposterous. It was not rejected due to a lack of documentation, insufficient financial support, an inadequate business plan, or even because the company did not have American employees (they had been hired and were already working). The refusal was based on the fact that the photos of his company's facilities showed several laptops but almost no desktop computers. The argument was that a technology company could not work with only laptops. It bordered on the absurd, Mr. Rodrigo believed. He had been working in the technology industry for more than thirty years.

I also thought it was a little odd, but I continued the meeting. I asked if he had kept a copy of the proceedings, and explained that the best course of action was to review all the paperwork so I could get a better understanding of what type of analysis was applied to the case. I told him that the process may have to be redone, but it would not bring additional costs since most of the documents could probably be reused. I wanted to visit his operation, so I proposed another meeting in his office where I could examine the documentation.

I arrived a little early to our appointment. I always had a somewhat investigative mind and wanted to check some things out, such as the type of building where the company was located and other details. Pretending I was lost, I spoke to a woman from another company, who worked on the same floor where my client had his office, and asked her if she knew anything about a new technology business that had opened there recently. Fortunately, I was able to get some answers. She showed me where my client's office was, and told me that she knew some of the staff that worked there, since they all arrived and departed at the same time each day. She also told me that it was a Brazilian company, with headquarters in Brazil, and that they had many American clients.

Well, I thought, it seems this is a company that's really here to stay and was committed to investing in this country.

I went to my client's office and was greeted by a friendly assistant. The premises were simple, but very tasteful. I observed that there were eight employees, busily working at their desks. They all had laptops, regular landline phones, and of course, the all too indispensable cell phones.

It all seemed pretty normal to me, considering that those are the exact same tools that I employed in my own work. Having a laptop often indicated that work was being brought home, but that was the way things were. Starting a new business required a lot of effort and dedication, I was well aware of that.

My client waited for me in a small but comfortable meeting room. He received me informally, following the popular Brazilian style of greeting, asking me casually, "How are you, Counselor?"

I replied, "I'm fine, sir. How are you doing?"

"Please, let's not stand on ceremony. After all, we're almost the same age, from what I can see. If you don't mind, can I just call you Francisco?"

"Of course, sir, I mean, Rodrigo."

We had a long conversation, because I wanted to review all the documents, obtain the information I needed to prepare the case, and analyze the rationale behind the denial of the prior application. Our meeting took two hours. When I left, I was feeling very enthusiastic about the case. I talked to Jennifer on the phone about our new client and went straight home.

It took me a week to prepare and send the application. In order to be thorough, I contacted large American companies involved in the computer industry. I asked them about the number of laptops that were sold to corporate buyers. I even asked about the use of laptops by their own employees.

The numbers surprised me. In more than one of those companies, the amount of laptop devices sold to corporate buyers accounted for more than 60% of the total production of computers. Basically, large organizations were using laptops on a regular basis, since desktop computers occupied more space and constrained mobility. I thought it made perfect sense. I obtained the exact sales figures, which the companies regularly released to the public.

I sent the application and the supporting documentation, including the sales report from the companies I surveyed. I only removed the photos of my client's facilities. Soon after, Jennifer answered a call from Immigration Services. The officer introduced himself as J. He was very polite, and went straight to the point.

"Good morning, Mr. Martins. I'm J, from the United

States Citizenship and Immigration Services. I have here in my hands an application for a work permit sent by your law firm, which has already been turned down twice by our Agency."

He continued. "The last application was denied because the company's facilities did not match what is expected of a technology company. What do you have to say?"

I thanked him for taking the time to call me, and then explained.

"Mr. J, I respect and appreciate the work you and your fellow officers do, and I'm certain that you conduct a careful review of all cases. I'm also certain that it's standard procedure to ask the opinion of experienced, qualified experts, when you need any technical support for your analysis, isn't that right?"

"Well," I continued, "My client's last application, prepared by another law firm, was denied under the explanation that his company, which is a technology company, mostly used laptop computers instead of larger computers. However, we believe that this is not a valid reason. As you can see, in the attachment number 22, one of the last attachments, we carried out a survey which demonstrates that, currently, most technology companies direct their own employees, as well as their corporate clients, to use laptops as their primary work tool. Basically, the reasons for that are twofold. First, there is the issue of portability. Desktop computers constrain mobility, which is fundamental these days. Second, there is the issue of space. Simply put, desktops require more space. Nowadays, laptop devices have the same capabilities and configurations as larger computer devices."

I took a deep breath and concluded.

"Therefore, I request that this new application be considered under the light of this criterion, since laptop computers are now highly used by all companies that operate in the technology industry."

After a few seconds of absolute silence, the officer answered in a very clear, assured voice.

"I had already examined those documents, Mr. Martins. But I wanted to speak directly to you, to make sure that your argument was well-founded, and to check that you really followed this case closely, and that you actually researched your client's work methodology."

He did not say anything else, only thanked me and bid me a formal goodbye.

I had a moment of doubt, and thought to myself, it's not going to happen. They won't approve this visa.

I was wrong, because two days later it was approved.

CHAPTER 22

New Commitments

Our situation improved gradually, as a result of our competence and professionalism. Typically, a new business, like ours, that starts out having only a small capital has to overcome an awfully heavy burden and exceed steep expectations. Essentially, the business needs to achieve self-sufficiency and get results, very quickly.

In the beginning, we even cleaned the office ourselves, because the money saved helped us pay the rent and cover our expenses. However, things started to get better, and since we were making a profit at last, we decided to hire a few employees. We were getting more clients, which created a new but welcome challenge: we needed to expand our facilities.

I was also able to move to a better apartment, which was tastefully furnished by Jennifer. We were even taking some weekend trips. Nothing fancy, of course. Still, we felt like we had the wind at our backs.

Shortly thereafter, we rented a whole floor in the same building where we had our office, which greatly facilitated our growth. Mr. Adams only came to visit us after everything was ready. I wondered why he did it, and once again, he demonstrated that he was still able to read my thoughts.

He walked around, taking in every detail, always with a smile on his face. When we sat in one of our meeting rooms, he finally spoke.

"You must be wondering why I haven't come before, aren't you?"

"Well, yes, sir, I am."

"It's simple. I didn't want to interfere with anything you were planning. I'm very impressed with your good taste. Jennifer managed to put a feminine touch in many of the details and in every room, which brings an elegant air to the office. The décor softens the austerity and coldness that one usually finds in a law firm. Indeed, your office looks cozy yet professional."

"Mr. Adams," Jennifer interjected gently, "You know very well that you wouldn't bother us at all, quite the opposite."

"Perhaps I wouldn't be a nuisance, after all. But I've always trusted Francisco's work, and now I trust yours. I was certain that you'd do an excellent job setting things up."

"But let's get to business," he exclaimed enthusiastically. "Time is money, and you'll need to work even harder to pay for all this." He smiled cheerfully.

"By the way, since we're talking about business, I'd like to inform you that I'm leaving our partnership. The firm is strong enough to survive without me. You don't need me any longer. Furthermore, I'll give up my shares in the firm, so you can keep investing in it."

My heart raced so fast, I thought it was going to explode right out of my chest. I had to take deep breaths to gather my wits and recover from this tremendous shock.

I quickly rejoined, "But, Mr. Adams, you don't have to do that. Things are going well, and our profit is increasing substantially. We can't let you leave our partnership without receiving the shares you're entitled to. That would be unfair, especially considering everything you've done for us."

"There is no injustice, Francisco. Consider it a gift to you and Jennifer, in recognition for your achievements. You can make it on your own, you know that. My involvement may have provided you with a sense of security, but it was your hard work and your focus that got you here and they'll help you move forward successfully."

I tried to insist, but he would not allow it.

Jennifer and I hugged him. When his arms enveloped

me, it was like I was holding my father so strong was the affection I felt for him. Needless to say, we were all very emotional.

This wonderful American, who had once opened the doors of his house to me, had opened the doors of his heart as well.

The days went by quickly. Our workload was always increasing, which made me think about my life and my relationship with Jennifer. We had been together for two years already, and I started to visualize our future and what I wanted for us.

Why not ask her to marry me, if we shared common interests, were moving in the same direction, and our relationship was deeply rooted in love and respect? I made my decision, and after a visit to a client, I went to a nice jewelry store and bought a beautiful engagement ring. I would ask her to marry me.

It was somewhat costly, and I would have to pay for it in installments. But one cannot put a price tag on happy moments. I never believed that happiness was a package that someone can just give you. As far I am concerned, happiness is an individual's work, without the participation of others, which means that our happiness does not depend on anyone else but us.

I always sought to retain in my memory the simple,

joyous moments in life, and make them last as long as I could. I would remember them again, and again. I would laugh at a joke, or at a story, more than once. It felt good to do that even when I was the target of the joke. I always had so much fun.

It has been said that there are many kinds of insanity in the world. Well, my insanity was to be happy and I did not want to ever find a cure for that.

I could not hide my excitement from Jennifer. She could see in my eyes that I was overjoyed and asked about it immediately.

"What's the matter, Francisco, have you won the Power Ball lottery?"

"Almost, my dear, almost."

"Just tell me what's going on!"

"What happened is that I looked for one thing and found something else. The client I met hinted at the possibility of referring our firm to a multinational bank. If they retain us, we can expand our work to other areas."

It was a half-truth, of course. The client did mention something like that, but I was euphoric because I had bought the ring. Obviously, it was not the ring itself that made me so happy, but what it could represent in the near future.

Delighted, she hugged and kissed me tenderly.

"Jennifer! If our employees see us, what will they think?" I asked smiling.

"That we love each other, silly."

A short time later, I found a pretext to go to New York. Mr. Adams was helping me organize everything. He was thrilled when I told him about my plans. Our excuse was that I had a meeting at the multinational bank, and Mr. Adams, who knew someone in New York who could help us in the negotiations, would go with me.

In reality, we were preparing a surprise for Jennifer. We had everything arranged, tickets, hotel reservations, and so on. We were setting everything up so I could propose to her. The day before our trip, Mr. Adams would tell us that he could not go, and would insist that Jennifer take his place.

Mr. Adams was very convincing, and Jennifer accepted the change of plan without any suspicion. Since our meeting was scheduled for Monday, we could enjoy a weekend in the city.

We arrived on Saturday morning, and after settling in to a comfortable hotel, we went for a walk. I had already made reservations for dinner at a very trendy restaurant.

Mr. Adams had helped me with everything. He not only suggested the restaurant, but also insisted on paying the bill.

Jennifer, who knew it was an expensive place, was surprised.

Even though she came from an affluent family, she supported herself financially, so she asked, "Don't you think this restaurant is too fancy? I know it's overpriced."

"You mean it's too expensive? Well, I don't think so. Besides, we never do anything fancy. We can give ourselves this luxury every once in a while, no?"

The dinner was spectacular. After the dessert was served, I prepared myself for the big moment. I got close to Jennifer, and started to open the box with the ring. But because I was terribly nervous, I opened the box too quickly, and as I was starting to pop the question, I saw the ring fall right on top of her meringue pie.

I always have been really clumsy. Feeling somewhat embarrassed, I said nervously, "Forgive me, it was supposed to be something special."

With tears in her eyes, she looked at me and exclaimed, "It couldn't have been more special, my dear."

I removed the ring carefully to avoid more disasters. Like a true gentleman, I got on one knee. As I knelt, I realized that it was an act of surrender. I surrendered to the charms of that woman, who had enchanted me with her love and her affection.

I looked into her eyes, and asked, "Jennifer, will you marry me? I'm a bit clumsy, but I love you."

"Yes, Mr. clumsy, I will!"

CHAPTER 23

The Excluded

O ur law firm was thriving. The monthly revenue frequently exceeded expectations, sometimes by more than 30% or 40%. We decided to review our organization plan, including the number of employees. We needed to expand our operations as soon as possible.

The firm started to focus on other areas of law besides immigration. It made perfect sense, since our work with immigration generated referrals to other activities. The results were great. We were doing as well in those other areas as we did in our area of expertise. Thus, we began to invest heavily in qualified professionals.

It was a sound strategy. We have never believed in the premise that an attorney can successfully handle all areas of law, like some sort of legal jack-of-all-trades. I believe in the old saying, "Every man to his trade." It is important to have a specialization. Those who want to embrace the whole world end up losing their way, and usually cannot embrace even themselves.

Our revenues were getting stronger. But we did not overreach. We did not want to rush into things and jeopardize everything we had done so far.

I was analyzing some spreadsheets, assembled by a capable assistant we had hired recently, and I noticed that our financial returns were becoming quite robust. Looking at them, I started to reflect about the importance of my work in my life. For a long time, I had experienced enormous difficulties, and in some moments, I even thought about quitting, a normal reaction for anyone who was going through that type of hardship.

But my faith in myself, and in God, helped me overcome those tough situations. They gave me the strength to get through my hours of desperation, when my perseverance, resignation, patience and my unshakable determination to succeed were most needed.

In those trying times, I could see that God works through us. The divine goodness is directed toward us, but because we are too anxious and worried with our daily lives, we are unable to see how much the Lord of life helps us at every moment.

I hardly remember Sunday Mass, which I used to attend with my mother when I was very young. However, one of

Jesus' teachings stayed with me. It was from Matthew 7:7-12. One day, I wrote it down and started to carry with me all the time. It says: "Ask, and it shall be given you; seek, and you shall find; knock, and it shall will be opened unto you. For every one that asketh receiveth; and he that seeketh findeth; and to him that knocketh it shall be opened. Or what man is there of you, whom if his son ask bread, will he give him a stone? Or if he ask a fish, will he give him a serpent? If ye then, being evil, know how to give good gifts unto your children, how much more shall your Father which in heaven give good things to them that ask him? Therefore all things whatsoever ye would that men should do to you, do ye even so to them: for this is the law and the prophets."

I reviewed my life over past years. I remembered the assistance I had received from my Cuban friend Mario when I had first arrived in the United States. Soon afterwards, I met Mr. Adams, this man I held in such high esteem, and who helped me tremendously. We were like father and son.

Jesus had really made a compelling and logical argument. If we want good things to happen to the people we love, without caring for anybody else, what about God?

My life was plentiful, and I could not only think about myself, Jennifer and our staff. It was necessary to do more and help people in need.

The Bar Association requires that attorneys take a certain number of pro bono cases each year. But I could accomplish much more. From then on, one day of the week would be exclusively devoted to providing free legal services to immigrants, no matter where they came from. We would, in some cases, have to break through some language barriers, but we would strive to assist everyone.

I talked to Jennifer about it and she agreed heartily. We shared the same core values about life and about our work. Those who have more ought to help those who have less. If humanity acted that way, then countless people would rise above the poverty line. If we all make the effort, people in need can be lifted not only from material misery, but also from moral misery, which is the worst of all.

The costs of this "Special Day" would be easily covered by our robust profits without impacting the employees' yearly bonus.

We explained our new initiative to the whole team, and they all agreed to the plan, without any reservations, which made me think we were all surrounded by divine blessings. I concluded that being compassionate is a wise thing to do, since the universe works in our favor when we open ourselves to our own goodness.

But I decided to keep those reflections to myself, worried that I would not be understood, or that I would be deemed a dreamer. The important thing is that we would have a great work to do.

I had felt, in my own skin, the anguish of being excluded. I had observed painful problems caused by the deportation of acquaintances. I had witnessed the break-up of families, mothers separated from their children, or from their husbands, and so on.

I have nothing against the law, or against the officers responsible for keeping and enforcing it. But I have heard individuals in positions of authority, as well as regular people, say that immigrants should be expelled as quickly as possible, because they are, for the most part, excluded from their own societies. However, the question I pose, in regard to people who defend those views, is this: who mows their lawns, services their pools, and cleans their houses? More often than not, they are immigrants, many of them living in the country illegally.

Plenty of talk, with very little

CHAPTER 24

Special Day

News about our "Special Day" spread rapidly. Every Thursday, which was the day we reserved to provide free legal assistance, the office got very crowded. We had to be well prepared to handle so many requests.

Easy cases were rare. We were like a magnet for complex, difficult situations. I always joked with the staff, and especially with Jennifer, "We asked, and God delivered!"

"Maybe He could have delivered a little less, no?" She answered one day with a smile.

"I think, Jennifer, that this is an opportunity for us to learn more about the law, and a reminder that we should never become proud, we must always be humble. Consider the people that came to us. Most of them are really suffering and going through terrible situations. One case is more challenging than the next."

"You're right, Francisco! Remember that guy that came in yesterday, with his two daughters, one was 6 years old, and the other was 10?"

"Vaguely. Yesterday was so hectic, lots of people to see. I remember that the older girl's eyes were red from crying. These are the people you're referring too, isn't that right?"

"That's right. I didn't have the time to tell you what happened. They're a young couple; he seemed to be about 35 years old, and told me that his wife is 32. They've been living in the United States for about six and half years. The younger girl was born here. They're in the country illegally. He worked as a gardener and she was a maid. They led a simple life. He told me they had gone through many hardships until they got here. They came from a Latin American country and crossed the Mexican border with the help of a *coyote*.[8] The only reason they were not caught by the border patrol agents was because the *coyote* used another poor woman as bait. While the agent dealt with her, they managed to slip through unnoticed."

"They had the older daughter with them? At the time she was just a little girl, wasn't she?"

"Yes, she was with them. She was about three or four years old. It was a quite an ordeal!"

---

8 A person who smuggles immigrants into the United States, typically for a high fee.

"But why would they come here if they had to go through all that?"

"It's like you always say, Francisco, 'A drowning man will clutch at a straw.' They were barely able to eke out a living. He was unemployed, and could only find a few odd jobs with the help of his friends, the type of jobs that did not offer any stability and that nobody wanted. She worked as a maid, but earned very little money. Since they lived on the outskirts of their country's capital, a part of her meager stipend was spent on transportation. Can you believe that?"

"Of course I do. That happens in my country too. Too much talk, too little action. Many promises are made when there is an election, but they're only empty promises, destined to be broken. If politicians had to actually fulfill their pledges, as people who make promises to God do, even God would get tired."

"You're always joking."

"If only it were a joke, Jennifer, if only ... but go on."

"Right. They settled briefly in California, and then moved to a town near Miami."

"They're very religious, and used to go to a church regularly. t's hard to believe, but they were denounced to Immigration Services by a fellow church member. According to Antonio, our client, the informant, whom he called a *cucaracha,*[9] was having problems with his immigration status as well, and decided to deflect the focus from himself by informing on others. At least, this is what other members of the congregation told him. Apparently, it was all part of some sort of plea agreement he negotiated with an immigration agent. But Antonio doesn't believe it, because the *cucaracha* owed him money and had repeatedly refused to pay it.

"How much did the informant owe him?"

"I don't know exactly, but judging by their situation, it can't be more than a few dollars. Antonio can barely support himself and his family. I felt sorry for them just looking at the clothes they were wearing, he and the girls."

It was clear that Jennifer was really touched by this case. She continued, "They panicked and left their house, carrying only a few belongings, but the wife was caught. She was detained, and is now waiting to be deported. He's very worried that eventually he'll get caught too. They're at a friend's house. This friend, of course, is also in the country illegally."

"What a drama, my God!"

"It is. But what really moved me was that he was in tears when he told me his story, right in front of the girls, who were crying too."

---

9 'Cockroach' in Spanish. Also used as a derogatory term

He asked me, in despair, "What am I going to do with my life, now? My wife is detained. My daughters are without their mother. I don't have a job or money. My friend is giving us shelter, but he earns barely enough to support his own family. It's one more burden for him to bear. My God, I can't even think straight! Why do they treat us as if we were criminals? The only thing we want is to work and earn our money honestly. Why do they dislike us so much in this country? Is it just because we're poor? Aren't we all children of God, like the pastor of my church always said? If that is the case, why do we suffer so much discrimination?"

"I told him to stay calm," Jennifer continued, "and that we'll do what we can. I also told him that our firm had worked on similar cases and we would see if we could find a solution for them."

"But Jennifer, you know that this is an extremely sensitive situation and there is nothing that can be done. His wife will be deported soon. How can we help those people?"

"I know, Francisco. But what else could I have said to him? The man was desperate. I needed to calm him down a bit."

"Of course, I understand. You did the best you could."

"Well, at the end of our meeting, I gave him some money, so they could at least eat something. The younger girl was complaining that she was hungry. What a heartbreaking situation! I felt terrible," concluded Jennifer.

Indeed, Jennifer sought to help them any way she could, but some time later, Antonio's wife was deported.

I made a point of going with Jennifer to give Antonio the bad news. He was devastated, wondering what he should do now that his family was torn apart. There was not much to say to that. Still, I reminded him how risky it was to live in a country illegally. Whether in the United States, or in another country, the danger was imminent.

But it felt like I was talking about pain to a patient with an open chest. It was downright cruel. He wept like a child. Tears fell down his sunburned face. It was one of the saddest scenes that I have ever seen. He tried to control himself, but was unable to. Jennifer was very emotional, and could not contain her tears either, while I got something in my eye, or worse, in both eyes, as I used to say when facing these situations.

We handled all types of cases on our "Special Day." But while they were very different, they all had, with rare exceptions, one thing in common: they were really, really tough cases.

To alleviate Antonio's pain, not only as a man, but also as a husband and a father, I offered him some money, which he could perhaps use to return to his country.

I was shaking from emotion when I wrote the check. He thanked me, and when he took it, I observed his calloused hands. I felt an immense sadness for that man, who had worked so hard, and yet had nothing, and now had to run from the country like a common criminal. I too had endured sorrow and misery, and that was why the plight of these wretched people spoke to me so loudly. I prayed to God, asking that He take pity on our smallness and our callousness towards the pain of others.

At that moment, I remembered a passage I had read about Mother Teresa of Calcutta. The reporter asked her what she thought science should invent for humans, and she brightly answered, "I wish, my son, that science invented a pill that cured indifference."

A few days later, Antonio's friend called Jennifer to inform her that Antonio had returned to his country, hoping that he could, one day, come back to the United States.

CHAPTER 25

Special Day – A Curious Fact

The so-called "Special Day" was becoming very interesting. Everyone in the firm got involved. Some of the attorneys even talked about having their lunch in the office so they could have more time for consultations.

One of the attorneys, who was a tad more religious than the others, suggested we start our activities with a prayer, asking for guidance and insight, to help us do our work effectively and have a productive day, a day that we all considered to be very special.

He said, "Mr. Martins, you know that our 'Special Day' is a charitable day. Well, Jesus is the greatest model of charity for humanity. In light of that, may I offer a prayer, as Jesus himself taught us to do?"

I agreed. Surprisingly, no one objected when the young

man made this proposal to the team. Like my friend and mentor, John Adams, his name was also John, he had recently graduated, and passed the bar exam with an excellent score. John reminded me of myself, when I was starting my career in Brazil. Modesty aside, he too was very decisive, and extremely persuasive when making his arguments.

So, on that Thursday morning, we prayed together, with John leading us in a respectful and engaging way. With a voiced filled with emotion, he addressed the Lord of life, more or less this way: "Lord, You created us as brothers, although we have not accepted it yet. We know little, but we know that we are all brothers in Your love. So, we pray that You enlighten our word, warm our hearts with Your blessings, and inspire us to apply the teachings of Jesus, who taught us to love our neighbor as we love ourselves. Have mercy, Lord, on our smallness, and guide us to assist those who seek our help, with insight and dedication. Let Your kindness toward us motivate us to be kind to others. We realize that our kindness is very little, because our understanding is very rudimentary, compared with Your greatness. But we are certain that You will help us overcome our limitations, because Your love is unconditional. We give thanks for the blessing of another day of work, which would be done not on behalf of others, but on behalf of ourselves, because we know, oh Lord of life, that when we help our neighbors, we also help ourselves."

His prayer, so simple and yet so genuine, moved us, and some of us, including myself, disguised our tears.

Jennifer, who never missed an opportunity to make fun of my soft heart – I have always been a very emotional person – looked at me lovingly, and remarked, "Have you got something in your eye again, Francisco? It's funny, isn't it? You always get something in both eyes and exactly at the same time."

"It's just a remarkable coincidence, Jennifer. Coincidences do happen, you know." I answered jokingly.

But a very curious thing was about to happen in my first client interview, on that sunny, gorgeous Thursday morning in Miami.

Our assistant walked into my office, accompanied by a beautiful young woman. To me, she looked American, so much so that I greeted her in English.

She replied in flawless English, and then added, "You're Brazilian, right?"

"Yes."

"Then you can talk to me in Portuguese, because I'm also Brazilian."

"Oh, I'm sorry, Ms?"

"I'm Ana. Ana Maria R."

"How may I help you?"

"Well, I'm a student here in the United States. I won a scholarship for an MBA, in a contest sponsored by the Brazilian university where I completed my degree in Business Administration. May I take some of your time, and talk about my life a little?"

"By all means. I'm at your disposal."

"First of all, I want to stress to you my desire to live here in the United States, permanently. I don't know how to explain it to you, but I feel like I've come back to my true home. I'm going to tell you a little bit of my story and why I made this decision."

"OK."

"I've always dreamed of the United States, literally speaking. Since I was a child, I had dreams in which I saw myself with my parents. Only, they weren't the parents I have today. I lived on a farm in Wisconsin, with my parents and my siblings. We raised cattle with the help of our staff. The place, people, and dates were always clearly revealed in the dreams. At that time, I was born in a typical American family. My parents had eight children, five boys and three girls. I was the youngest of all, the baby of the family."

"I was born on January 20, 1900. My name was Ann Marie G., daughter of Anthony and Melissa G."

Ana mentioned several names, including those of her brothers and sisters, offering so many details and with such clarity, it left me impressed. It was as if she were talking about her current life, only she could not be older than 25 years of age. I had read some of the writings of Carl Gustav Jung, exploring interesting psychiatric issues related to the matter, but what I was hearing, if it was not some bizarre invention from a very creative, or sick person, was intriguing at the very least.

But the young woman appeared to be a stable, balanced person. She spoke with such assurance and certainty, she convinced me that she was telling the truth. I was only 33 years old, but I had enough life experience to detect liars with relative ease.

It was astonishing, to say the least. I asked her some questions, and she continued to tell her story, as if she were narrating a novel.

"My father was a successful man, very respected in the region. He was the main supplier of a major company. Our farm was very productive, and as a result, our family enjoyed a good standard of living. I remember my first years at school, which incidentally is still operating at the same address. More than once, I got rewarded for being the best student in my class. My favorite subject was English, and I always got excellent grades in literature and grammar. That explains, I'm sure, why I always had an interest in this language in my present life. By the way, I'm sorry, Mr. Martins, but as you've probably noticed, I accept reincarnation as a logical and natural fact."

"You don't need to apologize, Ana. Please continue," I replied, unable to contain my curiosity.

"As I was saying, in my current life, knowledge of the English language has come to me naturally. Since my early childhood, as I was learning to talk, and began articulating more complex sentences, I spoke in Portuguese and English, simultaneously. My parents, of course, were bewildered. One day, they called an American woman, who lived near our house, and told me to speak with her in my "other language." That's because, in my naiveté, I used to say things, people, and situations always had two names, one in Portuguese and one in English. For example, I would say that a color was *verde* and green. That happened with every word I spoke."

She paused a moment and asked, "I hope I'm not tiring you with my story. Maybe you're thinking that there must be another explanation for those things, or perhaps I have some sort of genetic condition or something like that."

I replied, "Well, Ana, I can't say those possibilities didn't cross my mind. But I'm not knowledgeable enough to risk offering any scientific explanation, or to arrive at any conclusion whatsoever. Please continue."

"OK. My parents asked this American woman to talk to

me. She introduced herself in English, and we spoke for more than an hour, always in that language. I noticed that, from time to time, she exchanged glances with my parents, who were stunned, especially when I spoke about the places where I had lived in the past and how I had died."

"Ah. How did you?" I was so amazed, I could not resist asking.

"I was fifteen years old when my mother asked me to go to one of the corrals, and fetch a gallon of milk from a cow that was being milked. I didn't realize that the gate separating the corrals was open. There was a bull in the other corral, which my father had bought recently. I remember the clothes I was wearing, a bright red shirt and jeans. The animal, known to be very aggressive, escaped his pen and attacked me from behind. I didn't see the bull coming. I took a strong blow, and saw myself, in slow motion, as I was thrown against the wooden fence. I hit the fence so forcefully that when I hit the ground I could taste blood gushing from my mouth. Then, I felt a sense of weightlessness and watched the scene from above. I saw my body and all the blood everywhere. I also saw some of the workers running towards the spot, and my mother leaving the house to see what had caused all the screaming and the uproar. Someone told her Ann Marie had been in a terrible accident. The bull escaped its pen and attacked her."

She concluded. "At that moment, I lost track of time and space, and only become self-aware again at a certain age, in this present existence. Coincidences aside, even my name in this life is the same name I had in my previous one."

At that point in the narrative, I did not know what to think. She continued her story.

"But that's just a detail. When I came to the States, I had arrived three weeks before the beginning of my course, because I wanted to visit the place I saw in my dreams. With incredible ease, I located the city, as well as the farm, which still raises cattle to this day. The current owners are my former parents' grandchildren and great-grandchildren. I also visited the school where I had studied. I did it all by myself, without asking any help from anyone. I felt like my life was repeating itself, or better yet, that my previous life was as real as the one I have now. I wanted more information to prove my story and decided to search the local library. I figured that the accident causing my death must have been reported in the news. So, I scanned the old editions of the local paper. Amazingly, the accident was reported. It had really happened. I even saw a picture of myself. So, there it was, right in front of my eyes, the evidence showing that the features and details of my dreams were real."

I was speechless. If her story was just an illusion created

by a sick mind, it would be startling. However, if it was a product of her imagination, well, the girl sure showed a lot of creativity.

"What you have told me is really intriguing. Forgive my candor, but many people might find your story rather fanciful, don't you think?"

"Mr. Martins, I don't tell this story to everyone. I'm a convinced reincarnationist, but at the same time, I'm not worried about what other people think. But I'll say one thing: I don't just believe that reincarnation exists. It's more than that. I know it exists, which is very different. I know because I can feel that my story is real. I know because I found evidence that my story is real. I know because I have studied and researched reincarnation in depth."

She added, "I told you my story, first, because you gave me permission to do so, and second, because I think I should be as transparent as possible with my attorney. I believe that this is the basis of a good lawyer-client relationship, isn't it?"

Ana was very clever and insightful, and really looked like a typical American girl. I was amazed by her story. Whether it was true or not, I couldn't say, because I did not know enough about the matter to form an opinion, one way or the other.

One thing I have learned from Mr. Adams, in one of our

many conversations, is that we must admit our ignorance, when we do not know an issue in depth. Before we discuss something, we should be careful that we actually know what we are talking about, to avoid making an idle speculation. It reminded me of something one of my college professors once said, "Someone who speculates is usually irresponsible, since he has no idea what he's talking about, because if he knew, he wouldn't speculate, he'd be sure." They were simple, yet wise words. When we know a given subject in depth, then we can express our informed opinion in the matter, with correctness, and without doubt or prejudice.

Ana's history was fascinating. Still, I had not yet understood the purpose of her consultation. Thus, I tried to concentrate on the reasons that brought her to my office, and asked, "Well, Ana, what can I do for you right now, in your current life, so to speak?"

"Basically, I'm concluding my MBA at a University here in Florida, and since I'm the best student in the course, I was invited to work for a multinational company, which happens to be one of your clients. Since this company will prepare the paperwork for my visa application, I thought it was a good idea to have an early appointment with you and they agreed."

"I called your office, and when I got here, I learned

that my appointment was scheduled on the same day you conduct your free consultations. I don't know why this happened since the company will cover my legal expenses."

"As far as I'm concerned, Ana, our assistant made a mistake that brought about one of the most fascinating client interviews of my life. Rest assured that we'll attend your case with the care it requires. But I believe, or as you said, I know that life puts us in front of people that have something to teach us. As I told you before, I cannot judge without knowing all the facts, and even if I knew them, I wouldn't judge anyway."

Regarding the issue of judgments, I was always inspired by the passage in the Gospel where Jesus met the adulterous woman. He, who was in a moral position to pass judgment, considering his spiritual greatness, not only refused to do so, but took the opportunity to teach her a magnificent lesson, to go and sin no more.

We reviewed the paperwork for Ana's application, and after that, she thanked me and left, while I stayed on, meditating on how life is beautiful and full of intriguing surprises.

CHAPTER 26

Special Day –
Ethics Above All

Our "Special Day" attracted more clients than we could handle. To avoid postponing deadlines, or delaying procedures, we hired two contract employees.

On one of my consultations, I received a visit from a man, who looked around 40 years old, called Murilo S. He seemed to be a little anxious and agitated, so I sought to put him at ease, and hear his story.

"What can I do for you, Mr. S.?"

"Well, Mr. Martins. I've been living in the United States for a year or so. I came here as a tourist and never went back."

"You're living in the country illegally then. Why did you choose to stay in the United States, under those conditions?"

"The thing is, I made a small mistake in Brazil, and before I got arrested, I decided to move here."

"But a small mistake, as you say, would provide reasonable grounds for an arrest? Can't you seek another solution, instead of moving to this country illegally? Forgive my candor, but it seems to me that you escaped from one problem, only to find another one."

"Yeah. Sometimes we do stupid things, don't we?"

"It depends on the choices we make, isn't that so? Forgive me, but I have to ask, what was the mistake you made in Brazil? This information is crucial for your visa application."

"Well, I don't think it was that serious. Stuff happens, and if I did something wrong, it was because I was tempted to do so. I wasn't the only one to blame."

At that point, he began to sweat and to stammer. I did not want to put him on the spot. I just wanted to ascertain the facts, so I could help him in the best possible way. I offered a glass of water, and told him, "Calm down, perhaps we can find an appropriate solution for your case."

"I just don't know what to say, because the problem is happening here, too. Mind you, I cannot take the blame alone. It's not right. They're always tempting me."

It was all very confusing. I needed more information to figure out what the situation was, so I asked, "Who is tempting you, Mr. S.? Please, be more specific, and tell me what's going on, so I can assist you."

He told me his story.

"In Brazil, I lived in a countryside town, in São Paulo state. My neighbor had a daughter, who today should be around fourteen years old. The girl was always tempting me, making jokes, looking at me in a strange way. She seemed to be possessed by the devil. On a Saturday afternoon, her parents went out and left her alone. I told my wife that I had to go out and buy a spare part to fix my car, and managed to get into her house through the back door. She was sitting on the couch watching television. I jumped and grabbed her, before she could scream, and hit her on her face, hard. She fainted. When I saw her, unconscious and helpless, I was possessed by an incredible urge, and I had sex with her. I got out of there quickly, but while I was leaving, I saw that her parents were coming back. I didn't know what to do, so I fled, leaving everything behind. I don't think my wife, to this day, knows where I am."

He continued. "We had planned to take a vacation, and go to Disneyland. So, our passports, tourist visas and tickets to Miami were ready. I took my ticket, and luckily, I was able to get a seat on a flight that left that same night. I arrived in the United States with nothing but the clothes on my back, basically."

He concluded. "When I went through customs, the officer asked me about my luggage. I told him that the airline had misplaced it, and they would bring it to me at my hotel. I had some money, and managed to get by, somehow. I got a job in a restaurant as a dishwasher."

"Do you have children?"

"No, sir, it's just me and my wife."

I was shocked. He seemed to be a respectable man. What type of madness inflicted him? What a sordid, despicable tale.

"You told me that you made a small mistake. Were there other mistakes like that, Mr. S.?"

"Yes, once. But it was many years ago. The girl was probably the same age as the last one. But she was scared, and didn't tell anyone, so nothing happened."

It took all my willpower not to get up and punch him in the face. I wanted to beat him with something. I eyed a baseball bat a client had given to me, and thought it would be a great therapy to use it on him. It was a huge effort to contain my impulses. I tried to control myself, concentrating on the fact that I had in front of me a very sick man. I took a deep breath and asked, "Well, what do you want to do?"

"I hope you can help me get a work permit, so I can remain in the country legally."

A work permit? Help? My God, here I was, almost having a heart attack, and the man said he wanted my help! I was the one who needed help, to prevent me from wringing his neck.

I do not know what prompted me to ask him another question. I believe it was a divine inspiration. "Are you controlling your urges, Mr. S.?"

"Sometimes I look at the restaurant owner's daughter, who is about the same age as the other girls, and I can see that she's tempting me, she's offering herself to me."

My God, I thought, the guy is completely insane. He should be committed, at the very least.

I sought to keep a calm demeanor, to avoid scaring him. I took a deep breath, drank some water, and prayed to God for guidance because I did not want to say something that would offend him. But it took a huge effort on my part. I grabbed a pen and wrote down some notes, struggling to keep my hands steady.

"This is a list of some documents you need to provide, so that we can build your application, OK?"

"Yes, sir. Thank you very much."

I got rid of the man as quickly as possible. I did not shake his hand, because I knew I could end up throttling him instead.

I tried to regain my composure, and since I had never

faced a situation like that before, I decided to call my friend and mentor, Mr. Adams. I called his cell phone, something I disliked doing because he might have been busy and I could have inconvenienced him. But I could not wait. I had to talk to him.

"Hello, Mr. Adams. How are you? Can we talk?"

"Yes, Francisco. Is everything all right? Something happened to you? You sound worried."

I narrated the episode, as succinctly as possible, trying to hide my agitation. I kept thinking about those poor girls and what they had gone through at the hands of that madman.

"What do you intend to do about his last remark, regarding the daughter of the restaurant owner?"

"Report him to the police. But I might ruin my reputation on the issue of client confidentiality."

"It won't ruin your reputation, Francisco. On the contrary, it will enhance it, since you'll be preventing a possible crime. You know that."

"I agree, Mr. Adams. But you know that our competitors can be very malicious and willing to distort the facts."

"I'm well aware of that. It's a dog-eat-dog world, as you always said. But I don't need to teach you to be ethical, Francisco, because you have a good moral character already. Just relax, and do the right thing."

"I will do it, for sure! I just needed to pull myself together, and hear your opinion since you have so much more experience than I. I have never had to deal with a case like that before. I swear I wanted to strangle the guy."

"I can imagine, Francisco. After all, we're only human."

I thanked him, said goodbye, and contacted the police. Indeed, I felt at peace with myself, after the situation was resolved.

CHAPTER 27

A Big Family

I had arrived early at the office that Friday morning, which promised to be quite busy. I met Jennifer at the entrance of the building, also ready for work.

"How are you, Counselor?" I smiled, and gave her a quick kiss.

"I'm doing great, Counselor."

We opened the office, and started to chat about our future plans. Lately, I had been thinking about setting our wedding date and decided to talk with her about that.

"Jennifer, you know that our practice is going well, thank God. Our staff is as competent as we are. We work very hard and our revenue is increasing steadily. We could finance a house or an apartment and get married, what do you think?"

"Soon, they'll start accusing me of stringing you along," I added jokingly.

"I think it's a terrific idea, Francisco. Let's do it."

"Wonderful! Since we'll have dinner with your parents on Sunday, we could pick a date that is convenient for us, and break the news to them. What do you think?"

"I think it's best if we involve them in the choice of the date. You know how Mom gets her nose out of joint about certain things, sometimes even for trivial stuff."

"OK," I agreed, "I just hope she's resigned herself to my presence in your life, and won't have a heart attack when she hears about our wedding."

"How can that be, a *brazuca*[10] immigrant joining the family! Quelle horreur! Marrying an American?! Oh my God!" I said lightly, trying to imitate my future mother-in-law.

We both laughed a lot because we knew how to deal with Caroline, who deep down was a very good person, despite her tough demeanor.

On Sunday, after we finished dinner, we announced our plans. Jennifer's father was delighted, and thought that everything was great. He immediately agreed to the date we suggested, which was near his birthday on January 27.

As expected, Jennifer's mother, true to form, jumped from her chair, exclaiming, "Have you completely lost your minds?! It's too soon! Do you really think you'll have

10 An informal term often used to describe Brazilians living abroad.

enough time to find a home, furnish it, and prepare a wedding on such short notice?"

"Mom, it's the beginning of March. We have almost a whole year. Don't worry. It'll be fine." Jennifer countered.

"But, Jennifer! We need to notify the family, prepare the guest list, organize the ceremony, and do so many other things!"

My future father-in-law, knowing very well how that discussion would be settled, made some lame excuse and with a small gesture invited me out to the garden. He told me, with his characteristic unflappable demeanor, "Francisco, I've seen this movie many times before. They'll argue for about two hours, and in the end, Jennifer will convince her, as she always does. So, let's take a walk, it'll be good for our digestion, and for our health."

Jennifer did manage to appease Caroline, and after that first panic attack, everything went smoothly. My mother-in-law immersed herself in the wedding preparations, which was a blessing, because for the first time, I saw her enthusiastic about something that involved me.

We began our hunt for a home that met, if not all, at least most of our requirements, such as price, size, location, readiness, and so on. We relied on the help of a very good friend, a real estate agent. Knowing that we did not have much time, she made a pre-selection, and only took us to see the places that passed muster. Still, we spent a few weekends visiting buildings, apartments, and even some houses. Finally, three months later, we found a very cozy apartment, which fit our needs perfectly. We got a bank loan approved and closed the deal.

Caroline helped us choose the place, and after we received the keys, she and Jennifer selected the furniture and took care of the decoration. They both had very good taste and everything was arranged beautifully.

It was a rather interesting and fruitful period. I got to know my mother-in-law better, since we spent more time together. She was a great person; I always knew that.

As for Caroline, a mother knows when a man loves her daughter, when all is said and done, and I adored Jennifer. She had everything I had always dreamed of, such as a well-rounded family, a severe but also extremely affectionate and dedicated mother, and other simple things that I valued.

It has been said that when you have nothing, even getting one percent means a lot. But in my case, I went from zero to one hundred percent. I had nothing and then I found everything. I was deeply grateful to God, for blessing me with a wife and a family.

Our wedding was a joyous event. We gathered Jennifer's whole family, all of our friends, employees, and even a few clients we had gotten close to. Amid the celebration, I looked at my wife, and my new family, and wondered about the life I was building. At that moment, I remembered my father, and my childhood friend, Mr. Roberto, and wished they were there, sharing that special occasion with me.

I was very grateful to my parents. I knew that I owed them a lot, despite the difficulties I had experienced with my mother. She was a troubled woman, and had caused me a lot of pain, but she tried to do the best she could for me. I had been searching for her for a long time, to no avail. I wanted to provide her with a better life. But I would not give up. I would keep looking.

Feeling very emotional, I thanked God for my achievements and for my happiness.

We managed to take a week off, and went to the Caribbean for our honeymoon. The trip was a gift from our dear friend Mr. Adams, who was my best man at the wedding.

We embarked on our married life with much joy. Indeed, it was wonderful to wake up next to Jennifer every day. Her serenity brought me peace of mind and I was deeply grateful for that blessing.

A few months had passed, when unexpected news shook us to the core: Jennifer was pregnant! I was bursting with exhilaration and at the same time filled with panic. I was going to enjoy the fantastic experience of parenthood. Often, I found myself deep in thought, wondering what my life would be like from then on, and how I would face the challenges of bringing a child into the world and raising and educating him or her.

But life decided to bring me several challenges at once. Jennifer's first ultrasound scan showed that there were two little hearts beating in her womb. We were expecting twins! "Oh my God!" I thought at that moment. Instead of one, there will be two of them. Heaven must be having some kind of sale.

Before long, we learned their gender. They were a couple. Raising a boy and a girl at once would provide different types of fun, I thought. As for their names, Jennifer chose them: Robert and Claire.

The pregnancy was quite easy. Jennifer took every care to aid nature and to help our children develop perfectly, until at the expected time they were born healthy and strong. It was not because they were my children, of course, but they were gorgeous. Thank God, they looked like their mother.

A friend, wanting to be nice, told me, "Francisco, the boy looks like you!" Playfully, I answered right away, "Oh well, the important thing is that he's healthy."

Mr. Adams came to see us, accompanied by his family.

During a lively conversation, my dear friend and mentor told me, smiling, "Well, Francisco, you do like to work a lot, don't you? Besides having your hands full with the law firm, the clients, the staff, and all that running around, now you're a busy attorney and also a father of a large family. Who would have thought?"

CHAPTER 28

Happiness, Without Compare

I f there was one thing I could not say about my life, it was that it was monotonous. Between home, children, and work, my hands were full.

I remembered reading once, on a sticker on the rear window of a car, "Want to have a wild life? Have children!" My life was not exactly wild, but it was pretty eventful, for sure.

But perhaps that was what happiness was supposed to be, after all. The important thing was that Jennifer and I were very happy with our accomplishments and with our lives.

One day, I was having a friendly conversation with one of our clients, a man called Mauro Sergio, who exported fruits from Brazil to the United States. We were talking about family, and about getting used to new cultural challenges, when he asked me, "Mr. Martins, how did you adapt to the

226 | UMBERTO FABBRI

American culture, which is so different from ours?"

"Well, to begin with, I never make comparisons. Even in Brazil, when I had to make changes in my life, I avoided making comparisons. That's because we cannot find a perfect place in the world. If we keep comparing, we don't give ourselves the opportunity to be happy in the place we are living right now. In my practice, I met many immigrants who don't live here, and don't live in their homelands, so to speak."

I realized that my friend did not understand what I was trying to say, so I explained. "They're here, but they don't like it here. They really miss Brazil, and the family and friends they left behind. Yet, when I ask them why they don't go back, they say that they have jobs and enjoy a better standard of living in this country, so they can't just go back. Therefore, the big problem, for these people, is that they don't plant roots anywhere, they're always unhappy, pining for something else."

"But Mr. Martins," countered Mauro, "This is a very consumerist country, filled with cold and selfish people. Just look at the way they treat their own children. American parents frequently kick their children out of their homes when they reach 16 years of age, or so. It's a very different culture, and for this reason, really difficult to get used to, don't you think?"

His comment hit me like a kick in the gut, but I tried to keep myself calm. "What I believe, Mauro," I replied, "Is that we should avoid making hasty judgments, without really knowing the subject. To get to know a nation, one must live among its people, in order to gain a better understanding of their values, don't you agree?"

"What do you mean? Are you suggesting that our vision of the American people is distorted?"

"Exactly! Very distorted. Let's start by analyzing what a consumer is and what a consumerist is, OK?"

"Sure."

"Very well. We're all consumers, because we need to buy food, clothing, and other essential items, and pay for utilities such as water, electricity, and so on. Consumerism, on the other hand, is an imbalance that can affect people anywhere, not just Americans. The assumption that Americans -- and only Americans -- are consumerist is a stereotype, and does not match reality. I have seen people from all corners of the world afflicted by consumerism. Oftentimes, we blame the wrong people. People from all over the world come to the United States to shop, and why is that? Taxes here tend to be lower, which makes the price of goods more attractive. However, Americans are the ones that get the reputation for being consumerist, right?"

I realized that Mauro had not thought about that, so I

continued. "One day, I went to a mall with a Brazilian friend who bought 15 shirts from a brand that people here in the United States usually consider quite expensive. When I questioned my friend, he explained that with the same amount of money he paid for 15 shirts here, he would be able to buy only 5 shirts in Brazil. 'I'd fill my closet, and those of my two sons, for an affordable price', he argued."

"Of course, Mauro, this is a simple example. But I noticed that the same thing happens in relation to the price of automobiles, food, services, and so on. Can I make another analogy?"

"Go on."

"Beef production in Brazil is overwhelmingly export-oriented. My data isn't up to date, but it seems to me that 70% of the total production is exported, while 30% is directed to the domestic market. But who gets the blame for clearing forests and turning them into pastures? Brazil, right? However, who consumes all this meat produced in Brazil? Not the Brazilians, since they only get 30% of the production."

"But, Mr. Martins, you have to admit that there is too much waste here, don't you agree?"

"It was one of the first things I noticed when I arrived here, and it surprised me. However, over the years, I have realized that it was a misguided assumption. Basically, products have a more affordable price in the United States, as I mentioned earlier, and after some time or some years of usage, depending on the item, they become worthless, even for a donation, and are thrown out. Nevertheless, you will rarely see an American throwing away something that's still useful and in good condition."

"So," I concluded, "We must consider that our views can become quite distorted. For instance, you mentioned expelling children from home, right?"

"Yes."

"Well, I have two kids, and neither I, nor my wife, who is American-born, intend to expel them. We love our children. What happens, in my view, is that young Americans often seek to create their own space, which is extremely healthy, because it fosters their independence and stimulates the economy of the country."

"Mauro, an important point to consider, in this debate, is that the economy in the United States is much more decentralized, unlike Brazil. It allows anyone, a young adult, or a professional, to move within the country from one state to another seeking better jobs, or better academic opportunities. Thus, it's very common to see students who were born and raised in one state, to go and attend college in another. But usually they can count on the assistance of their parents, especially financially, until they can make it on their own."

"Evidently, if my kids enroll in a college nearby, they won't have to leave our house to live on their own. However, if they decided to study in another town, they'll have to move there, but it will be for practical reasons, because they need to live near their college, not because we don't want them in our homes anymore."

"Over here," I continued, "Young people are encouraged to be independent, unlike many families in Brazil and elsewhere, who do the opposite and keep their children at home. But those kids never cease to be adolescents, sometimes even when they're well in their forties; they remain in their parent's home and are often entirely supported by them."

"Mauro, nowadays I consider myself an American citizen. Yet I'm also Brazilian. I love Brazil, the country where I was born. It's my motherland, and I have the utmost respect for it. But I also love the United States. This nation welcomed me, and gave me the opportunity to become an accomplished professional. The American lifestyle has many distortions, for sure, but no country is perfect."

"If you allow me," I continued, "I'd still like to add one more thing, about family values. May I?"

"By all means, sir."

"I just want to express my opinion. I may be wrong, but

I firmly believe that, for a country to have such patriotic people, as they do in the United States, it's because Americans place a great value on the concept of family. To me, patriotism is a mere reflection of family unity. After all, what is a homeland, if not an extended family?"

It seemed to me that he did not like my speech. In any case, he did not appear to be persuaded by it. But that was only natural, since we cannot please everyone. The fact of the matter is that I do not have the habit of biting the hand that fed me in the past, or the hand that is feeding me in the present. What I do have is the habit of thanking God for all the blessings I receive, wherever I am.

CHAPTER 29

In Love

checked my schedule when I got to the office on Monday, and noticed that my day would be quite busy.

The first appointment, scheduled for 8:30 a.m., was for a man called Fernando H. and his wife, Renata. Although I had several commitments that day, including a few meetings, along with some important clients to visit, I always made a point to personally conduct the interviews for immigration cases, even outside our "Special Day."

When my assistant warned me, by phone, that the couple had arrived, I assumed they were older people due to the formal way she announced them. But when they entered my office, I realized that they were young, looking about 25 or 27 years old, at most.

As always, I began our conversation by addressing them politely, "Good morning, pleased to meet you."

"Mr. Martins," answered the man, "If you don't mind,

we'd like to speak in Portuguese, since we're Brazilians. Let's not stand on ceremony, OK? It is a pleasure to meet you."

"Certainly. It's Fernando and Renata, right?"

"Yes. Let's get straight to the point, to avoid taking too much of your time. It's about my green card application."

"Sure. What is your immigration status here in the United States?"

Fernando replied. "I came here to pursue an MBA. My parents have always invested heavily in my education, as well as in the education of my two brothers. My dad is a very successful businessman, working in the technology sector. I'm the youngest, and I was being groomed to take a position at our company."

He added. "But things never happen the way we expect, isn't that so?"

"It depends, Fernando. I believe that, most of the time, our free will prevails."

"Indeed, I agreed. But you know that the heart has its own reasons, don't you?"

"Sort of, Fernando, sort of," I answered, smiling, wondering what that was all about.

"Right. Well, my intention, initially, was to complete my MBA and go back to Brazil, as most Brazilian students do. But things didn't quite work out that way. I began to fall in love with this country, its people, its values and its culture.

Not that I don't like Brazil, mind you. Quite the contrary, I love my country. My whole family is there. We're very blessed, because we're really close and we respect each other, which doesn't happen very often."

I noticed that, although young, Fernando had very clear family values which, I supposed, was the result of the grounded upbringing he had received. It crossed my mind, at that moment, that a lack of education, and of values, is still a huge problem in the world. Educated people can make all the difference in the life of a nation. Incidentally, that was Jesus's mission, as far as I am concerned: to be a great educator of souls.

But it was time to stop digressing, and focus on our conversation.

"That's very nice, Fernando."

"Absolutely. I have nothing to complain about, honestly. But let's be brief. I met Renata at the university library."

At that point Renata chimed in, "That's right. I've worked at the library since I graduated. I was born in the United States. My parents are Brazilians, and share similar stories. When they were about three or four years old, they came to this country with my grandparents. They met at school at a young age, dated and married. They built a family here, and go to Brazil only on vacation."

"I met Renata at the beginning of my semester," added

Fernando. "We became friends, and eventually, I told her about my intentions to remain in the country. I also talked with my parents about my plans. They have always encouraged me to take charge of my own life, and do the best I could for myself. They just want me to be happy, on my own terms."

He continued. "Since we were little, I've heard my dad saying, time and time again, that parents cannot impose their notion of happiness on their children, because happiness is not a formula that can be passed from one person to another, but an individual construct."

"I agree with you wholeheartedly, Fernando. What's more, many times, we want our loved ones to abide by our own concept of happiness, and end up imposing our views on them, ignoring their individuality. It's not that hard to understand, basically. We are similar, but not identical."

I continued. "I remember a dear friend, who couldn't accept the idea that her son wanted to have a less lucrative career, when most of the family was very successful working in the financial sector. The boy actually tried to work in the family business, but after a while he abandoned it, and went to do what he loved most, which was to give tennis lessons. He's pretty happy, even though he probably doesn't make as much money as his family would like. I believe that life is too short to live in frustration. The fundamental question is, do I want to be rich, or do I want to be happy? Fortune and happiness don't always go hand in hand."

"A friend once repeated a very popular Brazilian cliché. 'Francisco,' he argued, 'Money doesn't buy happiness, but it buys you a ticket to Paris.' I thought about that and came to the conclusion that tears are tears anywhere in the world. The place we are at, and our socioeconomic status do not count for much if we are suffering. Thus, sweating is always better than crying, because while our sweat mostly comes from our work, our tears usually come from our pain."

At that moment, I realized that I was talking too much. It was time to get back to the matters at hand.

"I'm sorry, Fernando and Renata, but sometimes I talk a lot."

They both smiled. "We were told that, sometimes, you look more a like homeopathic doctor than an attorney. You know, those doctors whose consultations last for two hours or longer."

I was amused. If I were a physician, maybe I could find a medicine that alleviated my anxiety, which had always been pretty strong, I had to admit.

"Mr. Martins," Fernando resumed the conversation, "I discussed my plans with Renata, and she offered me the chance to remain in the United States."

"That's right," Renata interjected. "I told him that, if he wanted, I could marry him. Now, regarding this issue of marriage and immigration, I'm sure you're aware that there is a whole industry behind it."

"Unfortunately, yes. I'm well aware of that"

Renata, with a mischievous smile, replied. "Well, for my part, I'm completely against those illegal schemes. But I was already in love. I wanted to keep him here."

"She wanted to hook me!" Fernando exclaimed, laughing.

"What did you do?"

"We prepared everything," Fernando answered. "We had a few guests, took photos, and so on. There are people who actually sell this type of service."

He continued. "There is something I don't understand, however. I don't think the Immigration Services always see the whole picture. What I'm trying to say is that my father wouldn't have any problem sending money from Brazil to pay for my living expenses. He can pay for me to stay in the United States for many years."

I did not quite understand what he meant, so I remained silent, waiting for him to finish his thought.

"One of our family friends was an executive of a multinational company. His compensation package, plus his performance bonuses, made him quite wealthy. When he retired, he decided to live in the United States, but his visa application was rejected. It was an unfortunate decision, in my opinion. He would have brought all the money he needed to support himself in this country. Besides, he could have bought property and other expensive goods. Furthermore, he would consume services and pay taxes. In sum, he could have spent all his money in this country. The point I'm trying to make is that he would only bring money here, without taking anyone's job. But his visa application was denied because he didn't fit into any of the categories set by immigration law. To make matters worse, because of a reciprocal agreement between Brazil and the United States, he couldn't even apply as an investor, even though he had more than half a million dollars available to invest in anything he wanted."

He continued. "The way I see it, the standards are applied without considering the exceptions. I recognize the need for rules, or things will become a mess, but there are cases and cases. I'm not saying any of this to justify my decision to get a permanent residency through marriage. Despite enjoying a stable financial situation, I'm young and I want to work, like any person my age. So, in the end, it's possible that I'd occupy a job that could have been filled by an American. I'm just saying that the one-size-fits all approach shouldn't be used for immigration matters."

"Sometimes, Mr. Martins," he concluded, "I think that

Immigration Officers look at us, Brazilians, and think we're all a bunch of bumpkins. Perhaps they don't believe we have a vibrant culture, that we don't produce wealth, and that we don't have personal values. They have very low expectations for us."

"I understand what you're trying to say, Fernando. But I think those misconceptions won't last forever. Eventually, things will change for the better. We just need to give it some time. Patience is a virtue, right?"

"I sure hope so. Anyway, after the wedding, we started to live together. We had to keep up the façade, and pretend that that the marriage was genuine, because Immigration Services might investigate us. Since I had a good living arrangement, provided by my parents, Renata moved into my apartment. Of course, it was supposed to be only for a while to allow our friends and neighbors to see us together. But, as I mentioned earlier, she bewitched me."

"I didn't!" Renata replied immediately. "It wasn't like that. The truth was that he was falling for me too."

"I can't deny that I had a big crush on her. But initially, we got together because of my green card," Fernando replied, smiling. "Renata was doing me a great favor, without getting any monetary compensation, by the way. I've heard that those arranged weddings, on average, can cost up to fifteen thousand dollars."

"Yes. It's a pity, isn't it?"

"I agree. But as I was saying, we fell in love, and our fake marriage became real."

"What about your parents?" I asked.

"At first, both our parents disapproved of the idea. My dad got really angry at me, declaring that he had not raised a child with positive family values only to see him involved in an illegal scheme or a fake arrangement, which is the same thing, evidently."

"Right."

"However, things changed completely after they learned that what was supposed to be a simple ploy to solve an immigration matter had turned into something else. But there is more."

"What?" I inquired, with curiosity.

"Renata is two months pregnant. So, our parents backed down and agreed to our marriage. They're thrilled, especially because the baby will be the first grandchild on both sides. My mother and father are coming to visit in the next couple of weeks. Mom is eager to help Renata prepare the nursery, and she'll come back near the due date to stay with us for a while and give us a hand with anything we need."

Renata added, beaming, "My parents are also delighted, and promised to help us buy a house, or a bigger apartment, so the baby can have his or her own room."

I was enchanted by their case. It looked like a modern Shakespearean tale, without the tragedy, of course. A sensitive situation, which could have created some complicated legal matters, ended up as a love story instead.

Chance is really a funny, curious thing, I mused, remembering something I once read in the book *The Novice and the Pharaoh*, by the Brazilian author Hermínio C. Miranda, "Chance is but the pseudonym of God."

We arranged all the paperwork, and the permanent residency application was quickly approved. A few months later, Jennifer and I attended the christening of Fernando and Renata's beautiful baby girl, coincidentally named Jennifer.

CHAPTER 30

Life Story

I was deeply upset when I arrived at the office one Thursday morning. Due to the hectic traffic, an irresponsible kid with a recently issued driver's license hit my sports car. It was the car of my dreams, and I had just bought it four days earlier.

Unbelievable, I thought to myself. I spend a fortune buying a car, only to have a clueless kid ruining my pleasure. My intention was to enjoy my shiny new toy that weekend. I had planned a quick trip from Miami to Orlando, with a few friends, just for the pleasure of driving it.

The crash into the back of my vehicle was so severe that my car had to be towed. Meanwhile, the boy's car remained practically intact, getting only a few scratches.

It was our "Special Day," however, and I needed to pull myself together. My assistant announced the first clients of the morning. It was a couple, a man called Jorge M., and

244 | U<small>MBERTO</small> F<small>ABBRI</small>

his wife, Iolanda.

Seeking to get over the deeply annoying incident, I greeted them as cordially as possible. "Good morning, Mr. and Ms. M., how may I help you?"

The man answered. "Mr. Martins, we got married, and we'd like to ask you to prepare my green card application. Is that possible?"

"Yes, Mr. M., it's possible. Evidently, that means that Mrs. M. is an American citizen. Were you born here, or abroad?"

"I was born here. My parents are Mexicans. They crossed the border illegally several years ago, when they were still single. However, after a while, they were fortunate enough to be blessed with the generosity of some Americans who employed them as domestic workers. They sponsored my parents legalizing their immigration status. At that time, it was much easier to get a work permit than it is today."

"Indeed, things were different back them, no doubt about it," I replied. "What about you, Mr. M.? How long have you been living here?"

I asked this question believing that I might be facing a paid arranged marriage. If so, I was ready to send them packing quickly. Still smarting about my wrecked car, I was not in the mood to deal with any illegal scheme or unethical situation. I had had enough trouble for one day.

"We married eight months ago, but we didn't have enough money or time to prepare my documentation. First, we wanted to fix our home and organize our stuff. We want to adopt a child as soon as possible, since we are past the age of natural childbearing."

"I see. Your adoption plans are very interesting. It's a noble initiative on your part."

"Mr. Martins," Mr. M. remarked, "One day, when you have more time, I'll tell you my life story, and you'll understand why we want to adopt a child. Right, Iolanda?" He looked at his wife fondly.

Getting married to obtain a permanent residency is a common practice. Immigration is a complex process, especially for those who are in the country illegally, or those who do not have the required qualifications. But that was not the case with this couple, I realized. There was nothing fake about their union.

I am a curious person, I cannot deny it. Perhaps it's because my zodiac sign is Pisces. In Brazil, there is a popular saying that "The fish dies by its mouth, for being too curious." My client's life story could be quite interesting, and the subject of adoption touched me deeply. It was a noble gesture by those down-to-earth people.

"I'd like to hear your story, Mr. M., if you don't mind telling me, of course."

"I don't mind at all, but it was an unremarkable story. I'm just a regular guy, or perhaps I should say, Iolanda and I are regular people."

"Don't worry about that. A life experience is always rich, especially because one often finds beauty in the simplest things."

"Well, if you think so," He answered, and started to tell me one of the most inspiring tales I have heard in my whole life.

"I was born in a poverty-stricken town, in the Brazilian hinterland. I was left at the door of my future mother's house, by the grace of God. My adoptive parents had a modest background, but perhaps they were a little less destitute than my birth mother, whom I never knew."

"My parents worked and lived on a farm. It was an impoverished, hand-to-mouth existence. Almost every year, the crops were completely lost due to the prolonged droughts that devastated the region. But the landowner had a heart of gold. Knowing that the families working for him had nothing else, he allowed us to remain there."

"My father died as a result of an accident he suffered while working in the fields. He felt sick and then fell on top of a hoe. Probably, his fall was caused by weakness from hunger. His poor nutrition was insufficient to sustain his body, especially considering the backbreaking work he had to perform. The owner of the farm died shortly after, but since his heirs had little interest in the dry piece of land they had inherited, they allowed us to remain there to eke out a living any way we could."

"I was seventeen years old when my father died. From then on, I started to take care of my mother and my younger siblings. There were five of us. We endured a precarious, hardscrabble existence, in a badly depressed region that did not offer any hope for us. So, after much thought, I decided to try my luck in a big city."

"But luck, Mr. Martins, is the kind of thing you see a lot of in the movies and in the soap operas, because in real life, it doesn't just show up so easily for a kid who could barely read and write."

"After moving to the state's capital, I had no option but to live in the streets. My acquaintances, for the most part, were drug addicts, small-time thieves, pickpockets and prostitutes. I respected them, for my own safety, but I didn't get involved with any of them. I had little formal education, but my father always instilled solid moral values to his children. He was a strong positive influence on our character and on our behavior. My dad was a humble man who had a decent honest life. He led by example, staying out of trouble, and resolving conflicts peacefully. Furthermore, he avoided alcohol and drugs."

"I looked for work in the construction field, but I had no qualifications. My life became even more difficult."

"You can't imagine, Mr. Martins, how hungry I was. There were times that I knocked on people's doors, asking for a piece of bread. Some gave me food, but others shooed me away. Some people even sicced their dogs on me."

"Hunger hurts, and you can't soothe it. There is no Saturday, Sunday or holiday, it just keeps hurting and hurting."

"I know, Mr. M., I know." I replied.

"After a while, I found a job as a dishwasher in a restaurant. The owner let me sleep in the back, near the liquor stock. Then I finally started to save some money. One day, I heard a coworker say that he was going to try his luck in the United States, because it was a prosperous land, with plenty of money."

"I was intrigued and wanted to know more about it. After I learned how much money I'd need to travel and enter the United States, I decided to accept the challenge."

"We went to Mexico and then entered the United States with the help of a *coyote,* who took the little money we had, and used my two colleagues, plus a few other Mexicans, as bait for the border patrol. Perhaps luck was finally on my side, because while the agents dealt with them, I managed to sneak across the border."

"I was penniless, and didn't speak a word of English. I didn't know what to do. The *coyote* gave us a map, along with a compass, and a few instructions, so we wouldn't get lost. We had to walk through some remote areas and could easily be discovered. For that reason, we made our journey at night. So, I headed towards the town the *coyote* had circled on the map."

"I have always had a good sense of direction, and eventually arrived in a small town. Hunger was my constant companion over the next few days, until I met a Brazilian who was looking for people to work in the construction business."

"It was heavy work, but I got paid, and the company also provided lunch. Plus, they found me a place to live. I strived to learn some English, and saved as much money as I could. I needed to help my mother and siblings back home who were living in dismal poverty."

"Even in this country, I went through tough times. That was because I had to send money to my family, which needed it much more than I. But gradually, my life has improved. I got better at my job in the construction business, which has increased my paycheck."

"I was able to buy a house for my aging mother. She enjoys a decent life, thanks to the money I send her every month. I also helped my siblings finish their education.

They lifted themselves out of poverty, and improved their standard of living considerably."

"After a while, I met Iolanda, who works as a hairdresser, and after nearly two years of dating, we decided to marry. Well, you already know the rest."

I was speechless after hearing his story. There I was, upset and in a bad mood because of the damage to my car, in front of someone who had lived in bleak misery, endured many adversities, yet still maintained his dignity and hope for a better life. Life really teaches us. Often, we complain about the loss of our rings, ignoring those who do not even have fingers.

CHAPTER 31

I, Immigrant

ennifer talked to me about applying for American Citizenship. I had been very busy at work, and since I had recently renewed my green card, I postponed the application. Not that I did not find it important, on the contrary, it was a very special matter to me, and as such, I wanted to take my time and handle it carefully.

Eventually, I arranged the paperwork, and took the citizenship test, which evaluates the applicant's knowledge of the English language and American history. Everything went well.

Finally, the day of the oath ceremony arrived. To my surprise, Jennifer had invited people who had played a key role in my life in the United States and who were instrumental to my achievement and accomplishment. My Cuban friend Mario and Mr. Adams, with their wives, my in-laws, and a few other close friends were all there.

My wife knew how important that ceremony was to me. Not the ceremony itself, of course, but what it represented.

Shortly before the ceremony started, the memories came flooding back, one after another, in a retrospective of my life. I had faced so many challenges and overcame so many trials and adversities to arrive at that point in my existence. I felt like I was being awarded a badge of honor, the gold medal.

I had reached a fundamental milestone in my life. It was not just the issue of citizenship that filled my heart with jubilation, but the fact that this nation had welcomed me. In this country, I had met people who treated me with respect and dignity, and who believed in my potential. Many believe that the United States is the land of opportunity. Well, I certainly grabbed mine. It was not easy, but nothing worthwhile is easily achieved.

I felt very emotional when the officer asked me and the others fellow applicants to repeat the following oath:

"I hereby declare, on oath, that I absolutely and entirely renounce and abjure all allegiance and fidelity to any foreign prince, potentate, state, or sovereignty, of whom or which I have heretofore been a subject or citizen; that I will support and defend the Constitution and laws of the United States of America against all enemies, foreign and domestic; that I will bear true faith and allegiance to the same; that I will

bear arms on behalf of the United States when required by the law; that I will perform noncombatant service in the Armed Forces of the United States when required by the law; that I will perform work of national importance under civilian direction when required by the law; and that I take this obligation freely, without any mental reservation or purpose of evasion; so help me God."

Tears fell down my face. I was overcome by my emotions. I could not say a word. Only one thought occupied my mind: "I, an immigrant, was now an American citizen!"